THE BEST
WE COULD

A Memoir

ELLYN MANTELL

Content Warning: This book contains descriptions of child abuse, severe depression, and bipolar disorder and may be triggering for some readers.

ISBN: 978-1-966343-19-6 (hard cover)
       978-1-966343-20-2 (soft cover)
Mantell. Ellyn
Edited by: Amy Klein

Warren publishing

Warren Publishing
Charlotte, NC
www.warrenpublishing.net
Printed in the United States

To Michele and Mindy:
We are sisters, at times sharing one heart.

CONTENTS

INTRODUCTION: Overcoming Shame   3

CHAPTER ONE: Beach Days with my Father   16

CHAPTER TWO: Fridays with my Mother   24

CHAPTER THREE: The Music Man: My Father   30

CHAPTER FOUR: Little Girl Lost: My Mother   39

CHAPTER FIVE: My Grandmother: The Beginning of
Intergenerational Trauma   44

CHAPTER SIX: The Blue Baby Scale   54

CHAPTER SEVEN: A Fear of Police   61

CHAPTER EIGHT: Screeching in the Night   73

CHAPTER NINE: The Other Woman: Anita   80

CHAPTER TEN: Shouldering Responsibility   87

CHAPTER ELEVEN: Dinner with Donna's Family   97

CHAPTER TWELVE: Wake Up, Daddy   102

CHAPTER THIRTEEN: My Eating Disorder: A Way to Punish Myself   106

CHAPTER FOURTEEN: Getting Married   123

CHAPTER FIFTEEN: Fear of the Rabbit Hole: Motherhood   133

CHAPTER SIXTEEN: A Woman of Many Careers   145

CHAPTER SEVENTEEN: Major Surgery, Major Changes   149

CHAPTER EIGHTEEN: Rebirth   159

ACKNOWLEDGMENTS   167

INTRODUCTION
OVERCOMING SHAME

An indomitable human spirit ... is it something with which one is born? Or does one learn not only to survive but to thrive?

How wonderful it is to state that yes, I have overcome my shame. As a woman well into my seventies, I am grateful to share with you that my lifelong struggle with self-hatred and negativity about my person and my body is in the past. It has taken a lifetime of perseverance and determination, but looking back, every bit of effort has catapulted me further into the life I have wanted, one of joy and success rather than pain and suffering. I have created the nuclear family I always wanted, enjoy loving relationships with my two sisters, and treasure friendships and bonds with my extended family. I have a healthy relationship with my body, no longer hearing the denigration my mind so often whispered in my ear. I have replaced my revulsion with pride. I have licked my wounds, healed them, and with the coping methods I have discovered within myself, I will not allow anyone to pick at the scars that remain. I feel empowered to know that my parents did what they could, my sisters did what they could, and I did as well.

This is a memoir of becoming well again, since I was not born with negative feelings about myself. Those feelings were learned. Mine is a story of second chances to find all the goodness life has to offer and, most importantly of all, to recognize that I was loved. My story is also an homage to the concept that each of us grows from an amalgam of so many elements. Many of my elements were difficult to overcome, but I know my strength and determination. I appreciate the power I have found within myself, my spirit, my fight, and my bravery, as well as my ability to help others in their time of need. I do whatever I can to enable those who may benefit from what I have learned. That drive is key to my own survival and, when I allow myself the luxury of focusing on it, fills me with pride. Had I not grown up with my parents, I might not have known any of that existed within me, which may just be my superpower! So there truly is a yin and a yang to everything. Our goal as humans has to be to grow from all that comes our way.

Still, awakening in the middle of the night, as I so often have, I find myself smoothing my nightgown as I walk to the bathroom. Regardless of my age or growth, I can't help but feel the slap of my mother's words: *Your lower body is bulky. Your legs are short and stubby, like your father's, and you waddle like a duck at times.* Humiliating! Similarly humiliating was the nickname my father gave me: Itty Bitty Titty, for my small chest. (He gave Michele and Mindy, my two younger sisters, nicknames that were no more respectful or comforting.) Looking in the mirror, I see my mother's deep-green eyes and her broad smile, which startles me, since how could I smile as I remember the pain, the hurt, the sadness, the thousands of *what ifs*? These *what ifs* encompass years of *What could have been?* Yet I am grateful to my mother for giving me the greatest gift: appreciation for the mother I had because she led me on the path to become the mother I have always wanted to be.

Both of my parents were mentally ill. According to the myriad of mental health professionals with whom I have worked, my mother likely suffered from borderline personality disorder, and my father, bipolar disorder. In contrast to many others who struggle with mental illness, my parents were also abusive and unable to control themselves. They hurt my sisters and me over and over again, unwilling to see their own part in the overwhelming sadness that blanketed us, blanketed our family. My parents each arrived at their marriage with a host of emotional challenges, and their challenges only escalated from there. Together, they were combustible; it didn't take much to cause an explosion.

In my fantasies, I often wonder what would have happened if my mother had told my father that she would not tolerate him crawling into bed for days, even weeks, at a time. Of course, he would have gone to bed anyway. That was all he knew to do when faced with overwhelming stress, tension, or the combative energy erupting from their interactions. It was how he ran away for whatever period of time it took to resurface, ready to face the demands of family life once again. Or sometimes, in my reverie, I imagine him standing guard at the door of our bedroom, like the brave marine he had been, preventing her from pulling my sisters and me out of sleep, deep in dreams, awakening to her fingernails digging into our warm flesh, forcing us to clean out our toy chest. In these imaginings, my parents look at each other, and us, and see what could have been a family composed of parents who guided, assisted, shared, mentored, and worked through problems with dialogue rather than punishing silence. Instead, speaking with words of love, not humiliation. In my imaginings, when one is unable to cope, the other knows how to soothe their three daughters with words of confidence and encouragement, love and softness. A fantasy, a beautiful fantasy.

I was no more than three years old when my father placed me on their big bed, pulled down my underpants, took off his belt, and used the strap on my bare skin, two or three times, as punishment for some infraction of which I have no memory. What could a three-year-old have done to deserve a strap beating? As he hit me, he told me it hurt him more than it hurt me. My husband Bruce would *never* do that, but had he even showed *intention* of hurting either of my daughters in that way, I would have grabbed her and run for the door, slamming it in his face. I would have laid down my life to protect my girls! My mother, however, would rather have had my father attack me than her.

In reality, the dance my parents performed was just that, their own dance, but my sisters and I felt its collateral damage. Michele, Mindy, and I grew up experiencing shame, neglect, sadness, secrets, sadism, loss, and abandonment. For much of my life, I felt the sting of not being loved. Like my sisters, I wanted to be cherished and treasured, wanted and secure, yet those comforts, like stability, remained elusive in our home. My parents only rarely considered our emotional needs, so consumed as they were with their own.

My sisters and I grew up in a time of silence about most diseases, a time when mental illness was one to be particularly hidden. The world we grew up in also hid abusive behavior. My family lived within that intersection of mental illness and abusive behavior, with limited to no coping skills other than screams or silence. Even our neighbors probably had no awareness that the family next door, the one with the three cute little girls and the car that frequently sat in front of the house all day, for days, and the beautiful mother who often walked around as if in a trance, kept countless secrets. My friends assumed I wasn't gracious enough to invite them to our home, never imagining that my parents considered such visits taboo.

Today many people who live with mental illness, including borderline personality disorder and bipolar disorder, are able to learn new and healthy behaviors with treatment and support. Yet my parents lived in a time when treatment for mental illness was often stigmatized, unavailable, and ineffective. Our society vilified many people with mental illness as criminals. How could any of us have spoken of such people in our own families?

I now feel fortunate to live in a time when treatment for mental illness is more effective and accessible. Yet cultural and economic pressures can still perpetuate stigma and inaccessibility. I am a mental health advocate, and I want you to understand the vital importance of destigmatizing mental illness, making therapy accessible to families, and reaching out for help when we are struggling. I think it is an optimistic and important viewpoint to maintain—with therapy, people with mental illness can become effective parents. I believe that healing takes effort, learning, and community. It is important to acknowledge that my parents did not experience the support and treatment I have worked hard to secure for myself through my own story.

My father was sad and pathetic much of my life, when he wasn't sadistic, cruel, and abusive. My mother was needy, chaotic, violent, and physically aggressive. The volatility of their relationship was ever present, and living within their sphere was a constant danger. However, as I enter this last part of my life, I have decided that their very act of preserving our family, challenging as it was for them, spoke to how much my parents loved my sisters and me, even as their actions were not loving. While their intentions and their desires might have been to show their love for us, my parents did not have the skills and behaviors to put their love into action. Still, my parents could have left my sisters and me. But they didn't. They chose to keep us together.

My sisters and I have relied upon and devoted ourselves to one another. That is a unique and lifelong gift, one we greatly appreciate, one whose abundance cannot be overstated, one that has breathed life into us count-less times. We have stood upon one another's shoulders to fight whatever battle needed to be fought. We have always had one another, and that is how we survived. As you will read, on the day of my wedding, had my sisters not been there with me, for me, I would have had no wedding gown to wear. I knew I could count on them to support and uplift me, as my mother was enveloped in her own importance, unable to put my needs first. Even on my wedding day, she was the mother—I was only the bride. The same gown that my mother threatened to cut up with scissors if it came into the house was altered later for each of my sisters to wear, as well as a cousin and stepsister. I look back on her threat to destroy something so important to me and wonder how she felt as it became equally important to others as well.

As the eldest sibling, my role in the family continues to be protector and storyteller, and I have many stories to tell. Although they are mine, these stories also reflect the lives of my family, from my grandparents to my parents and sisters. I have always known on some level that I was different, that we were different from others, but it was while I was walking to school one day in March during my sixth-grade year, Michele home sick so she was not in my charge, that I told myself there would come a time when I would write my story. What never occurred to me until now is that I believe my parents never realized, or perhaps even imagined, that our family lived a life in contrast to that of others. They had no idea that violence and hostility, pain and suffering, misery and degradation were not part of the human experience for everyone, but were for us. Instinctively, we never shared what we lived, but I cannot help but wonder what others thought?

I know that many who have experienced trauma self-hide and never share their story. Perhaps I am more open to this "telling" because I have experienced such challenges with my health, have an ileostomy, am a national advocate and mentor for other ostomates, and facilitate ostomy support groups. In our meetings, we have conversations that are deep and meaningful, open and revealing. I have felt the physical and emotional benefits of these community gatherings where no subject is off the table. So I hope that by sharing the story of my childhood and adulthood, I can help guide others in healing from their trauma.

There were times when my parents connected with my sisters and me and times when I felt we were objects in the ocean, floating farther away from their shore. Today my parents feel simultaneously larger than life and smaller than the mouse named Squeaky my father created to keep me from crying when I was scared. My parents spoke in booming voices and sad little whimpers. They screamed and cackled, cried and whined, begged, pleaded, distorted, and prayed; this is the cacophony of sounds I hear when I remember them. Their behaviors were erratic, unreliable, and predictably unpredictable.

I have read that the ability to trust is one of the first achievements of a child. How could my sisters and I have possibly learned to trust when up soon became down, and down just as quickly became up, and tomorrow everything might become the opposite again? The same mother who cared for me when I was eleven years old and nearly comatose from the measles-induced unheard-of temperature of 107.1 was the same mother who often forgot me at school, then slapped me with a vengeance once she remembered and raced over to find me crying on the steps of the closed building in the dark. When one of my therapists asked me why I had ever thought she would pick me up before dark, I sadly, softly stated, "Because I had hoped I was worth remembering."

The father who cried when I broke my collarbone, taught me to dance on his feet, arrived early at my high school performances to get a seat on the aisle, loving the flirtatious attention he received as the dancers and singers walked to the stage, and applauded loudly, seemingly filled with pride for his daughter, was the same father who tormented me for weeks that he wouldn't be attending my sweet sixteen—it wasn't important enough to him—knowing he broke my heart each time he told that to me, then waltzed in as if it were normal to abuse my adoration of him. I was shocked when my wish for him to attend came true, but instead of feeling joyful at my party, I sobbed so much that I remember nothing else from the celebration. Just like my mother, he was unreliable and predictably unpredictable.

My mother, sisters, and I once donned our best dresses for a "Cousins Club party," having been excited for weeks in anticipation of seeing my father's side of the family. Our dresses were ironed, our shoes clean, and accessories at the ready. My sisters and I took pains to look our best, knowing how much pride my father took in our appearances, and were eager to see many cousins our own age. Walking down the stairs into our living room, I looked at all of us in the big mirrors on the wall, and I remember thinking that we were a stunning family. Then in one millisecond, something occurred that changed my father's expression. Perhaps it was something one of us had said, or my sisters and I had giggled as teenage girls might do, or else it was some other phantom infraction that resulted in his taking off his pants, hanging them on the closet door, and getting into his bed. The four of us cried and begged with disappointment—but also with resignation. Why would we have thought the story would end any other way?

My father, when he was depressed, slept as much as two weeks at a time, filling our house with a morgue-like pall. As the pungent odor of sleep shrouded the house, my mother, so in need of his love or touch, would first throw a tantrum, lying on her back, flailing her legs and arms like an insect, and screaming for him to awaken. When that brought no response, she would bite the back of his calf while he slept on his belly, drawing blood as she attempted to rouse him from his stupor. I didn't realize it at the time, but those bites were also foreplay, which frequently ended with him jumping up and chasing her around their bedroom until their sexual coupling followed. They had such explosive fights, the car became our safe place, and that was where the three of us found solace, even a place to sleep. At other times, we heard their battles ending in loud sex. So involved were my parents in their own lives, they wouldn't have thought of closing the door to their bedroom.

There were other times "under the big top," as I refer to it, when after a week of leaving us for the security of his bed, my father would awaken at 2 a.m., blow reveille on his clarinet, and make pancakes for us, smothering them in butter and drowning them in syrup. Joy filled the kitchen! And then, CRASH! We may have had a warning, or none. We may have counted the days and anticipated the change coming, or not. We may have noticed our mother gathering her negative energy and picking a fight or vice versa, either of which would send him to bed. All we could do was watch, and wait.

Many have told me over the years that I am "always in gear, ready for the next step." It may be annoying to them, I suppose. But that is how I was trained—to always have a backup plan, think ahead. My survival and, at times, even my sisters' depended upon it. While my friends were studying for tests or socializing, I was spending precious energy anticipating the next crisis. Turning off that inner voice and telling myself I do not have to go back in time, only forward, has been a huge challenge for me. I do my best to stay in the moment and fight the conditioning of always being ready for the next challenge. But there are times when I fall back and roll down the hill, attempting to stop myself from hitting the bottom. Those are the scary times because I lose my self-confidence, which has been so hard to attain! Like any other addict, it is too easy to do what is familiar, even as we know it is wrong for us.

To this day, I have a heightened awareness of potential dangers and need to prepare for every possible future event, frequently causing a knot in my stomach. I anticipate all that could happen, that may never happen. My sense of responsibility for everything has me contemplating and mobilizing resources, even when I know they are unlikely to be necessary, so trained am I to deal with any or all potential emergencies or events I was taught to believe were emergencies. New situations present me with an even greater need for preparedness, as I reminisce picking up the pieces of a childhood experience that caused a battle between my parents. I saw myself as the referee, always ready to separate them. Or else, I would take responsibility for whatever transgression took center stage …. "Daddy, I stole the dollar from your pants; I'm the culprit. I was a bad girl, and I am the one who deserves to be punished. Please wake up, and I will never do it again." Did he know I was lying, that it really wasn't me? I suppose it didn't matter. If he awakened, I had done my job.

My parents' fights overflowed into my daily life. Their physical violence caused nightmares in which I could save them, even as my hands and arms bled from pulling them apart. I still pull back, recoil, when someone approaches me in a manner that puts me on alert, anticipating being attacked, needing to protect myself. It is so reflexive, this arching my back to ensure my face is out of danger, my mother never having the self-control to not hit or pinch that which was in front of her.

My erratic mother was unstable, easily frustrated by my sisters' and my own maturation into young womanhood, a natural part of separation.

She felt betrayed and attacked by our developing relationships with others and needed constant reassurance that we loved her, even as she withheld her love. Any disagreement with her opinions must have felt like a terrible assault to her, as such histrionics and vitriol would surface. She had the most difficult time allowing us to move out into the world and took our growing independence as a personal rebuff. She frequently told us that her happiest days were when we were toddlers; she had loved to polish our white shoes and iron our dresses, which I had loved too, clearly feeling an abundance of nurturing. But then she would let us know that she had done so much for us and we had never appreciated her enough, as if enough was ever enough. As the eldest, I fought hardest for independence, yet I fell apart when she did, so difficult was it for me when she felt I had betrayed her. I tried to have bravado, I truly did, but I loved her and didn't want to hurt her. My intestines reacted to her sadness, her anger, her hostility, her anxiety.

My parents' words and deeds still fill my nights, and sometimes my days as well. This I want to share with you: It would have been easy to look at myself as scarred and defeated, relax into similar behavior, and abandon the fight. I could have identified as the eldest daughter of two mentally ill parents—what can anyone expect of me? In fact, it would have been much easier than the rope I had to climb, arms burning from the effort, to rise above the twisted filaments of fibers of my parents' reactions and tutelage. I didn't want it, and I couldn't stand for it! I wanted something so different. My vision of my life, my family, my place in the world needed to be defined by my character, my determination, and my undying willingness to do what needed to be done to get there, regardless of how high I had to climb out of the pile of ropes which anchored my feet.

My mother and father fit together like pieces of a puzzle, interfacing and interlocking their pathologies. What they did to keep my sisters and me together was miraculous, of that I have no doubt, but surviving was challenging for all of us. There are times when I find it impossible to believe it was all real. But it was real, the legacy I have protected until now. I have written this memoir to share my story and share the road I traveled to arrive here. My sister Michele reminded me I have been writing this for decades, and in my seventies, it must now be finished.

The "me" of today I want you to meet is loving and loved, yet aware of the sadness and disappointment I experienced as a child. My parents were ill; they were fractured and lost. They found each other, and that is quite miraculous. They created our family, knowing no other way to live, to survive. There were days that were hellish and days that just were.

I have worked hard, seeking a great deal of support, guidance, therapy, and awareness. Thankfully, I have been able to create the family I wanted and chose. But it took an enormous amount of energy, tears, physical and emotional effort, and pain. Each step in therapy brought me closer to understanding myself. When I added medication, the picture sharpened for me, came into focus. And the more I did for others in my mentoring and advocacy work, the better I felt about myself. Today, my therapist speaks to my growth when she continues to point out that I am mentally well and have healthy relationships with my husband, daughters, sisters, and extended family and friends.

The final piece of my story is this: I am proud to say I loved my parents! This pride comes from the recognition they did the best they could with the skills they had. I believe that if they could have done better, they would have done better. The behaviors that stripped them of their happiness did the same for us. These lessons were not easy for me to learn or to absorb. For years I wanted more from them. It is only now that I realize I received the most they were capable of giving, and that is enough. I speak for myself but believe my sisters share some of my feelings. It is one of the worst feelings in the world when a child learns their parents are tainted; children thrive on the pride they feel for their first ombudsmen. Yet, like going to an empty well, we could continue to do so or realize that the well will never have what we need to quench our thirst. That is a fact, unable to be changed. We have had to learn that, absorb that, own that.

My memoir is meant to show the consequences of childhood trauma and acknowledge how challenging it is for families to make the behavioral changes necessary to build more complete and fulfilled lives together. Yet with the right tools and coping mechanisms, better lives are possible. I believe that today there is so much more awareness and understanding of mental illness and how families transmit trauma across generations. Hence, treatment feels almost compulsory since it can make such a difference. Together, treatment, community, and love can help us break the cycle of intergenerational trauma.

Lacking a mothering model in my own mother, I looked to my mother-in-law, Eleanor, for guidance. She taught me so much, and her love created a path for me to follow in mothering my daughters. "Family comes first" was Eleanor's policy, and "Being a mother is the most important job you have," she would say. She was always affectionate with me and the girls. Holidays and family dinners were her gifts to us, and she prepared elegantly. But even that was so difficult for me because I never felt that I measured up. Eleanor and I spoke every day, and if I felt I had said something wrong, which I very often felt, I would call her back and apologize. She would admonish me, telling me I said nothing wrong. But my self-censor was so acute that I criticized myself over and over again, always angry at myself for any words that didn't sound positive and upbeat. I was terrified of losing her approval, her love, since I assumed that was always a possibility. I was so used to the feeling of begging to be loved, one infraction and it was over.

The funny thing is my mother-in-law teased me saying that I saw the world through rose-colored glasses. Nothing could have been further from the truth. My vision of the world was dark, humiliating, and denigrating. Yet she brought light to me—and to my daughters. Allison and Emily loved spending time with her and staying at her house, which was warm, comforting, and organized, totally contrary to the house where they stayed with my mother those few times. I would do anything to maintain that beautiful connection Eleanor had with my daughters, anything! My daughters only visited my mother for me, to save me from my mother's anger and her jealousy, but they hated every minute.

I had made myself into a pretzel, always trying to do better for others, not for myself, every day a reaction to those around me. I made Bruce my judge, always looking to him to see if I was enough, if I could have done better, if I could have said something in a different way, always scoring my behavior, always carrying him in my back pocket, ready to tell me whether I had succeeded or failed. How exhausting for him, and how self-loathing of me. For a long time, my need for acceptance kept me from developing my own inner dialogue and my own personality, even my own belief system. My daughters could have been angry at me, a mother with such low self-worth, but their memories are, fortunately, of the times we shared and experienced together and how I showed them they were loved and treasured. I am eternally grateful they feel this way, eternally grateful I made their maturation something normal and to be embraced and admired.

Today, I am a wife, mother and mother-in-law, grandmother (Gummy Ellyn), sister and sister-in-law, and daughter-in-law. I am also a friend, mentor, advocate, writer, and motivational speaker. I rise to challenges and speak for those who need a voice, such as my ostomy community. In fact, this is my second book. My first, also from Warren Publishing, is entitled *So Much More Than My Ostomy: Loving My Perfectly Imperfect Body*! I encourage reading it if you or someone you love has an ostomy. I wrote *The Best We Could: Healing from Intergenerational Trauma* to find peace that comes from recognizing, sharing, and healing intergenerational trauma. To the young Ellyn, who knew she would write her story someday, I have done so, and it feels liberating. Now that I am sharing my life story, I seek to uplift others who need to heal from intergenerational trauma and speak for progress for our mental health. Perhaps my story will help other individuals face and survive their own childhood traumas, or at least know they are not alone. I am forever grateful to imagine my story has meaning to others. By writing this book, I have become everything I have ever hoped I would be: a woman who loves and appreciates her family and friends, an advocate, a writer, and someone who can finally make sense of a life that has never made sense and find value in all I have learned.

CHAPTER ONE
BEACH DAYS WITH MY FATHER

On Sundays when the heat in our small apartment became particularly oppressive, my father took us to the beach. His pitch-black hair was damp with sweat on those days, and my mother stayed in her baby doll pajamas long after breakfast.

Our apartment was tiny, with few windows. Condensation danced on the panes of glass on those extremely hot days, the heat of the bright sun radiating through the light curtains. The rooms, all painted a grayish white, were small but ample, and we were grateful we no longer lived with my grandmother and the rest of the family. We had a living room, dining room, kitchen, and one bathroom. My two sisters and I shared one bedroom, and my parents slept in the other. We couldn't afford air conditioning, although my parents had a window fan. There was little furniture, just beds and dressers, a kitchen table, a sofa, and a small television in the living room.

By May each year, the days could be so stifling that my sisters and I couldn't go out to play—even our pink Spalding ball held no interest. Sweat was visible through all of our shirts, even as none of us actually did anything.

On this particular Sunday, I was seven, Michele four, and Mindy one. The minute my father mentioned the Shore, my organs twisted and turned in an internal fight between fear and joy.

Going to the beach meant my father was in a good mood, so we smiled and hugged him, praising this gift of generosity. He had been asleep in his bed, their bed, for days, and after this bout of depression, he was now awake. That put a smile on my mother's face. I felt it was my responsibility to do all I could to keep her smiling and make my family happy. I hugged him at his hips, starved for his attention and affection. We all responded with signs of adoration for this loving gesture.

I gathered matching bathing suits for my sisters and me, choosing the purple, yellow, and pink plaid with ruffles around the straps. We kept the bigger beach towels under my bed, and I shook them out before handing them to my mother. But my favorite part was selecting the "nighttime clothes" for after our showers. As young as I was, I loved putting outfits together for my sisters and me, and I included sweaters for the nighttime chill. We didn't have many garments from which to choose, but I did my best. I even packed our hair brushes, rubber bands, and bobby pins. My mother made the tuna salad sandwiches and filled the thermoses with tap water.

We lived in The Stuyvesant Village, an immense, sprawling apartment complex that rambled into two counties in northern New Jersey, with our particular apartment located in Union County. These hundreds of one- and two-bedroom apartments were carved out of farmland and built for the soldiers returning from World War II who were eager to marry, start families, and make up for time lost to war. In 1954, the housing was affordable and well populated. There was a laundry room that serviced many apartments with its six washing machines and dryers, although many of the women preferred clothes lines. There was a playground somewhere in the complex, but we never went. We heard stories of strangers hanging out there and that the sliding board was rusty and the merry-go-round unsafe. Our bedroom window, on the first floor, backed up to a dairy farm, and it was not unusual to hear mooing or see a calf looking into our apartment for its mom. I wept at times for the calf, knowing it was lost and sensing that it might not feel loved by its mother, just as, many times, I didn't feel loved by mine.

From our home, the Jersey Shore was a ninety-minute drive on the back roads that would eventually be replaced by the New Jersey Turnpike. My sisters and I anticipated the bumps and rattling of the poorly constructed roads, and my eyes closed as we approached each and every rattle.

My parents' fighting began within the first mile. It was part of the fabric of our day; I knew that at any minute, one of them would start an argument. They fought about the Camels my father chain-smoked, which seemed to absorb most of the air. What air was left was acrid, awful. He shouted that he needed to smoke to stay calm during the long trip with three little girls who squealed and giggled and couldn't stop touching and taunting one another in the back seat. My mother used the long drive to remind my father what a failure he was, how he rarely worked and there was little money. In return, he said that she was stupid and couldn't even keep the ketchup bottle clean. How would any of us become wives when our mother was so bad at being one, he wanted to know. My parents' need to hurt each other was always present. Our day at the beach had just begun, and already I felt anxious and helpless. "Stop! Stop! Stop!" I yelled, though I wasn't sure if the words escaped my mouth or stayed only in my mind.

When we finally found a parking spot, our forced march to find the perfect beach spot began. As my father insisted, it could not be too close to the ocean, where a rogue wave could drench our things, and it could not be too far, as we would burn our feet on the way to the water. Setting up the chairs, blankets, coolers, towels, and umbrella took him a while, the cigarette constantly dangling from his mouth, his huffing and puffing reddening his face. I feared he would explode. Once we had claimed and arranged our spot on the beach, my sisters started to dig in the sand and search for shells—although Mindy was very young, she followed Michele and attempted to do everything she did. As my sisters played, I remained alert for arguments. These arguments could have all or nothing to do with us, the heat, the sand, the water, or even the people next to us on the beach.

I would try to distract my father, usually the one to turn angry first, or my mother "swooning" in the sun. "Take us to the water," I would beg, my tone letting him know he would be our hero. I never learned to swim and was terribly uncomfortable in the ocean, but I would do anything to defuse the hostility growing stronger as the day progressed.

Looking back, I felt it was my personal responsibility to be prepared for battle at all times, and my parents' battles were easy for me to anticipate. Whenever I sensed that a fight was about to begin, I searched my mind for a way to deter it, but my memory is that I wasn't very creative; I would simply cry and beg my parents to not fight. "Please, please don't fight!" I would whimper, dissolving into a miserable child. Sometimes, my actions helped ameliorate the conflicts between my parents, while at other times, my parents simply ignored me. Either way, I stayed constantly vigilant, and I was willing to become whiny, childlike, and irritating. Sometimes, when I felt no other options, I would kick at the sand, making a mess around our chairs.

Years later, as a mother, I rarely wanted to go to the beach. My anxiety about the beach stemmed less from remembering my parents' fights than from the overwhelming vigilance that seemed to grow in my mind. I simply could not relax as I anticipated some catastrophe that I could not foresee or control. Fortunately, Bruce was always "all in" the few times our family went to the beach. His actions and ability to take over if necessary showed me he knew it was difficult for me and would help as much as possible. Yes, I was worried about the ocean, the waves, the sun, the sand, but the girls loved it, and still do—to this day, the beach is one of their favorite places to be. My daughters played by the water, me overseeing; they sunbathed; they had fun. But I could not relax until everyone was showered and dressed and ready for dinner and the rides. By then, we were closer to leaving, ice cream cones in our hands, my vanilla-orange swirl cooling my roiling insides.

Sometimes, my father picked me up and, holding me tight, took me to the edge of the water. Thrilled and scared, but loving the rare attention,

I nuzzled into his strong neck. Hiding my fear of the water, I screamed with what appeared to be delight but was actually terror. I knew that at any time, my father would drop me in the waves. Alone in the water, I exhausted myself, flailing and begging for help. It was my challenge to return to my father, but there were times when I simply felt myself sinking under the water, saltwater in my lungs, my heart racing, my eyes rubbed raw from crying. He just stood there watching. Eventually, I felt his arms or, occasionally, those of another person trying to help, lifting me from the tide. My father expected me to be grateful for learning to ride the waves, so I thanked him, over and over again, my heart pounding. I may have struggled in the waves, but I quickly learned to pretend in order to bask a bit longer in his attention. That attention cost me my confidence. To this day, I am terrified of the water, and I have never learned to swim.

Trips to the beach were trials by fire. My hair was the darkest brown, but my skin was porcelain white. Back then, conventional wisdom held that sunburns were a necessary step to building a tanned "base." My skin never tanned, however, and only suffered second-degree burns and blisters. Every trip to the beach ended with a trip to the pharmacy to find something to soothe my seeping wounds. Typically, the pharmacist suggested calamine lotion for the glaring red eruptions. What he didn't say was the lesson my parents needed to learn: *Keep this fair-skinned child out of the sun!* While I understood that each trip to the beach would cause me to burn, I never objected or screamed in pain. I didn't know I could. I knew three things: I must be a good girl, find a way to make my parents and sisters happy, and show constant appreciation for every bit of love or support my parents offered us. I still grapple with making people happy to the exclusion of my own happiness. I suppose there will never be a day when I don't. But I continue to work on my awareness and remind myself I am entitled to advocate for myself.

In contrast, my own daughters seemed to learn at a young age that if they spoke respectfully to me, they could say whatever they needed to say. I encouraged them by valuing their feelings and helping them feel safe when they told me how they felt. I have no doubt that Allison, my eldest, would have screamed at me had I ever left Emily to burn as my parents had left me. And perhaps, had my parents failed to protect my younger sisters, I would have screamed as well. But sadly, as a child, I had neither the ability to protect myself nor feelings of entitlement to do so.

Today, as a mother of adult daughters, I often ask permission to speak freely. I believe one of the greatest threads that connect the three of us is our commitment to communicate with awareness of how the receiver of the message may feel. I might also add that both of my daughters are excellent communicators, trusted for their concern for and ability to support others. Allison is a school social worker and educational consultant, and Emily, among many things, is a master-certified executive coach. Communication is their great strength.

As the sun began to set, my parents, my sisters, and I packed our belongings in the trunk of the car and entered the public showers, my father on one side of the building and we girls on the other. Inside, plastic curtains separated the long lines of showers. My sisters and I jumped around in the cold water pouring from the tin faucet, happily washing off the sand and sun. When our family reunited outside, my parents looked fresh and elegant. My father had donned a crisp white shirt tucked into navy pants, and my mother had poured her tall, willowy figure into a starched shirtwaist with a high collar that reached only halfway up her long, slender neck. My mother braided Michele's wet hair and put clips in Mindy's curls. I was proud I could make my own ponytail, which squeaked with dampness as I brushed it and twisted the rubber band. My sisters and I wore our sundresses, again matching, this time in a floral print. Together, our family looked like a Coppertone ad, the perfect family after a perfect day in the sun.

Back in the car, the fighting immediately began again. "We waited so long on line for showers because you wouldn't leave the beach early," my mother snarled at my father. "You were too busy listening to your radio, another baseball game."

My father screamed over her that it was enough that he had brought us to the beach—she should be grateful for once. "Nothing is ever enough for you," he yelled, a familiar rebuke. I knew his words by heart!

When we arrived at Evelyn's, a seafood restaurant that fed children for free, we waited on another line. My mother was famished and cranky, having subsisted on black coffee all day; my father was always ready to eat. They began to jab at each other, sometimes pinching each other's arms. Mindy cried. I rebraided Michele's damp hair to pass the time and try to coax my mind away from the pain I knew would follow.

At Evelyn's, we always ate fish sticks and french fries, and vanilla or chocolate ice cream for dessert. It should have been a child's dream meal. But lemon wedges accompanied the fish sticks, and lemons had become my torment.

The first time I received the "lemon treatment," I was five. Right before our ice cream, my father softly told me to switch places with my mother and sit next to him, a delightful command that promised me a moment of closeness. Looking back, I misjudged my father's demeanor. What I thought was softness was actually sadistic seduction.

As I snuggled to his side, my father plucked a lemon wedge from the glass dish and grabbed my sunburnt arm. In a flash, his dark eyes twinkling and his lips smiling, he squeezed the lemon juice, pulp and all, onto my blisters, holding me tighter as I screamed and struggled. I was in shock. He was in his glory! Oh, the pain I felt then! And the betrayal!

"Stop squirming," he growled.

My welts swelled to the size of a quarter, burned, and made a fizzing sound I can still conjure in my mind. For days they seeped and ached as I wondered how my father could have caused me such excruciating pain. Why would he do that to me when I had always tried to protect him, to show him my adoration? How could he have hurt me with a smile on his face?

Each beach outing ended with the lemon treatment at Evelyn's. So as we waited in line, my stomach and intestines twisted, and my heartbeat quickened. But I showed no fear. When I was a young child, the sadistic side of my father, his cruelty masquerading as concern, terrified me. Yet as I grew older, my terror transformed into a determined numbness. I knew he wanted my terror, my cowering, and my sobbing. So I refused to give him all he wanted. I couldn't allow myself to give in. When I was a teenager, my father would promise to pick me up from a party, then he would simply say no when I called to ask for a ride. No—as if there were a choice for a parent! "No, walk home." In the dark, alone, as a young woman. He didn't seem to care when I walked into the house. So I too pretended that this experience was normal and that I was fine.

Looking back on my father, as I have countless times, I realize his love came packaged in his need to cause pain, perhaps to ameliorate his own, maybe to even feel something. Perhaps no one ever showed him how to love. Perhaps he was simply numb, as I too became.

I was the eldest child, the one who idolized him, and he was confident in my adoration. But he took me to the darkest place. The man I adored, the man who was supposed to be my protector, the man for whom I would have done anything in the world to show how much I loved him, caused me such enormous physical pain, and even more emotional pain.

No matter how prepared I was, my belly lurched whenever he said, "Come sit by me. Hold out your hands."

CHAPTER TWO
FRIDAYS WITH MY MOTHER

Every Friday afternoon, my mother would drive to her hometown of Irvington, New Jersey, and begin her Shabbat ritual.

She would pick up a standing order at the Chancellor Bakery for a large round yellow birthday cake covered in thick chocolate-fudge icing with pink, yellow, and blue flowers ceremoniously circling the cake and "Happy Birthday, Leah" (her Hebrew name for Lillian) written across the top in Barbie-pink script announcing her weekly birthday celebration. This weekly order also included a sugar-free apple pie and a loaf each of pumpernickel and rye breads, sliced thin.

Next, she meandered over to the deli that had been owned by her aunt and uncle decades earlier and was now owned by another resident of the town, to pick up two slices each of American, Swiss, and Muenster cheeses. Finally, she floated to the candy store next to the deli. There she filled up a small brown bag with penny candies: two each of Tootsie Rolls, caramels, root beer barrels, cinnamon discs, small packages of M&M's, and Mounds candy bars. She topped off her shopping spree with one piece of wrapped bubble gum. Back in the car, she needed to look at herself in the mirror in order to congratulate herself on her accomplishment. This weekly ritual gave her a great sense of satisfaction. She rarely allowed us to accompany her on her shopping expedition, but my sister Mindy did from time to time. It was my mother's time, and hers alone.

My mother was beautiful by anyone's standards except her own. She had dark-green eyes, high cheekbones, and a slender neck. No longer its natural honey color, her hair was now light blonde, as was the look of the day, and always perfectly coiffed into either a teased pageboy or flip, depending on her hairdresser's mood each Saturday. From time to time, I went with my mother to the salon, where I found myself mesmerized by the process: shampooing, wrapping her shoulder-length strands in large rollers, drying, combing out, and spraying. In the end, she looked like a movie star, gushing with gratitude at the portrait Mr. Robert or Miss Patty created for her.

She had a shapely, well-proportioned figure, which she whittled from time to time with exercises she watched on television, carefully following Jack LaLanne's instructions. She had a height of close to five foot six to accompany her pinup-girl figure. Her small waist and narrow hips needed little firming, and neither did her long legs. Her greatest feature, and perhaps greatest attribute, however, was her smile. She had the most inviting smile I have ever seen in person, one that illuminated her stunning face.

Sadly, my mother never saw these gifts. She saw only the mottled skin on her legs due to what she called "poor circulation." (Perhaps the true cause was Ehlers-Danlos syndrome, a connective tissue disorder rampant in our family.) Her feet were size 9, which humiliated her since she thought women should have small feet—she often referred to herself as an oaf. Of course, at her height, it would have been inappropriate for a woman to have any smaller size feet. Yet since she believed the size of her feet made her unfeminine, she bought her shoes at least a size smaller. Her vision was poor, but she refused to wear glasses, so she fell frequently, tripping over sidewalks, not noticing items on the floor, all because she couldn't see where she was going.

Approaching home after her food-shopping expedition, she began to show the rush of adrenaline for the ritual that was to come next. Her coloring changed, more heightened, cheeks glowing, her movements more balletic, her shoulders relaxed, her jaw less tight. Trancelike, my mother entered the kitchen, where she had already set the table for her party. First, she slowly unwrapped the cheeses, as one would undress a lover. Next, she used her thumbnail as a measurement to cut a corner from each of the slices. She placed each triangle into her mouth as though it were a holy sacrament wafer. She never chewed, but simply let the soft food dissolve on her tongue.

Then she placed a similar-sized corner of each of the breads into her mouth, letting each piece dissolve into a mash that needed only a chew or two before being swallowed.

Next, she sliced a quarter of the apple pie and placed it on the awaiting salad plate. She slurped the sweetened pie filling off a spoon before scooping the apples into her mouth.

Then came the birthday cake. Candles were at the ready to circle the cake, always three: one for the birthdays she had never celebrated as a child, one for the present, and one for good luck. Singing "Happy Birthday" to herself, she placed the candles in their customary location, dead center in the bull's-eye of the cake, as if she were positioning the point of a compass before drawing perfectly round circles. The wedge she cut out of this cake was large, necessarily so, in order to have all colors of flowers represented. It was so large that it required another, larger plate to accommodate it. After eating the inside of the wedge out to its frosted edges, my mother put down her fork.

She most often performed this ritual by herself, dimming the lights so that she was almost in the dark. Somehow, my sisters and I knew to leave her alone; somehow we had learned that this was her time to tame her sadness. When I reflect on those eerie feasts, I understand that, of course, I must have been frightened—my mother resembled an apparition, almost as if she weren't there. She reminded me of Miss Havisham in her jilted wedding scene, surrounded by a dessert table of decaying cakes.

My mother's belly already looked distended, but she was not yet satisfied. Opening the bag of candy required the most concentration. She lined up the pieces like little toy soldiers. She ate one of each, comforted by having another to eat if desired, and waited a few minutes before opening the finale, the single piece of bubble gum, which she chewed for a while. Her face grew soft as she blew large pink bubbles, the bigger the better. I often wondered if the bubbles ever burst, covering the sides of her hair; they were that big. She was in a trance, in a world I knew I could never reach.

After she finished eating and bubbling, my mother rewrapped the remaining cheeses in their waxed paper and threw the packages into the refrigerator, where they shriveled, discolored, and dried until they ended up in the garbage, usually by the following Wednesday. The breads sat on the counter where, from time to time, my sisters and I secretly nabbed slices to make a sandwich or toast. Bread was on our list of forbidden foods due to its caloric content, so we considered it contraband and, thus, surreptitiously stole it. My mother always warned us, "A moment to the lips, a lifetime to the hips." She closed the birthday cake into the large box that had enfolded and protected it. After tossing last week's "Happy Birthday, Leah" cake, shrouded in frost, into the garbage, she placed this week's box in the freezer. She buried her bag of candy in the bottom of the trash can. I suppose she felt she had to hide any signs of joy in her life in front of my father. Their interaction was, it seems to me, one of misery and abuse, anger and judgment.

The apple pie, however, found the most bizarre resting place of all. My mother placed the tin of leftover pie, uncovered, under the front seat of her metallic-blue Cutlass. When I began to drive and needed to adjust the seat, I frequently found my hand dripping with apple filling. The first time this happened, I cried. I cried with the awareness that my family was terribly different from others, and that at seventeen years old, I could no longer pretend it was not true. After that day, I always kept tissues in my handbag. But what good would it do, I wondered, to dwell on the knowledge that this was my mother? I already felt so different from other young women as it was, and the need to hide one more secret only added to my fear that I was blemished, badly blemished.

After her Friday afternoon eating ritual, my mother began Shabbat morning guilt-ridden and inconsolable. I too felt deeply sad and unsettled. It wasn't only from knowing that the haphazardly wrapped leftover cheese, symbolic of her love-hate relationship to food, would rot until someone discarded it; her self-flagellating was even more frightening.

She covered her head with a long black mantilla (actually, a lace tablecloth), stood at the open kitchen window, and begged G-d for forgiveness. Muttering and swaying, she swore, "I will never do it again!"

Her words made me believe that G-d cared about what she ate. Maybe he also cared what I ate. As I watched her davening, hitting her chest, bobbing her head, sniffing, sobbing, and pleading for help with never eating her comfort foods again, I wondered how she had transgressed against G-d. If her eating food was a transgression, then what hope was there for any of us? We transgressed constantly. Was G-d angry at us? Would we be punished as well?

My mother's prayers were answered—temporarily. All week, she survived on black coffee and hard-boiled eggs. She was the picture of penitence and willpower—until Friday came and she began her Shabbat ritual again.

My mother constantly spoke of her "all or nothing" personality, which may have reflected her borderline personality disorder. Food was the number one measurement of her belief that she should either eat or starve; have it all or have nothing; deserve cake, pie, candy, and bubble gum, or only black coffee and hard-boiled eggs. Growing up, I was hungry or guilty so much of the time that it took me decades to learn to develop a normal relationship with food. Between my "waddling like a duck" and having a combination of my mother's thin, narrow upper body and my father's short, stocky legs and wide rear end, I always felt awful about my body. My parents never seemed to have an awareness of how hurtful their words, their inferences, or their tone made us feel.

Fortunately for me, I jumped on the jogging bandwagon two weeks after giving birth to Emily. My friend had told me that jogging was the source of her weight loss and tight body. Even though I was nursing Emily and rather top-heavy, I went out and ran around the corner that night. The next day, I ran two times around the block, and an obsession was born. I would like to think this was a healthy obsession because the more I ran, the less interested I was in what I ate. I began to realize that the food, what I ate or didn't eat, was less important than the noise in my head about it. As running and other aerobic exercises quelled that "conversation," I began concentrating on healthy eating, fueling my body, not punishing it with food, or lack thereof.

My daughters have always seen me exercise, and they too have followed my example. Their children have the same desire to stay in shape, and I would like to believe that the healthy goals we all pursue grow from a good place, not from the pathological place I saw in my home when I was growing up.

Bruce and I take our commitment to exercise seriously, making it a part of our daily routine. Fortunately, so many of our generation do the same; for us, exercise isn't a burden but fun. I love speaking with my daughters as they head to yoga or to walk, and as I head to my Pilates or biking. What a difference in attitude—food is not punishment, exercise is not punishment, and taking care of ourselves is the goal. With exercise, we have created a healthy coping method for our emotions.

CHAPTER THREE
THE MUSIC MAN: MY FATHER

I adored my father. He made me think of music, especially when we danced, me upon his feet, his arms holding me tight. Those times were exquisite, and they were mine. In my dreams, he was my "Music Man," filled with great passion for singing, dancing, and playing the clarinet. It was true; he encouraged me to feel the pulsating rhythms of Glenn Miller, Louis Armstrong, and Duke Ellington. Even as a young child, I would jitterbug as if I had lived during their era. I was guaranteed attention from my father as I slapped my thighs around the dance floor, my mother's bright-red lipstick wetting my lips, towels stuffing the shoulders of my blouse. For years, I was his devoted minion, able to identify every band and song of the Jazz Age.

For decades I couldn't understand how this wondrous man could go from twirling me around the dance floor to becoming an immovable lump, moody and dark, bathed in despair, in bed for weeks at a time. What was the force that dragged his thunderous spirit from his being, sapping our family of his ebullience? Now, from the mountaintop of adulthood, with sorrow, I know it makes perfect sense.

Herman (Hy) Aron Finkel was born into a family cloaked in mournfulness. His sister, Helen, was several years older than he, and a baby named Aron had been born a few years before. Aron had a devastating appearance; he was born with a cleft palate and lip, and unable to be fed, he was left to die.

That was our family lore. Today I believe that my grandparents' shame must have catalyzed their decision to withhold nutrition from Aron—or perhaps they wanted to prevent Aron from being placed in an institution. No doubt, my grandparents, Minnie and Michael, had no desire to draw negative attention to their part in the large dynasty who were very well respected in Elizabeth, New Jersey.

Like most in their affluent and influential family, my grandparents were well-heeled. There were dozens of Finkels involved in real estate, butter, and eggs, and eventually, some of the family took advantage of the country's dependence on oil to form a successful fuel company. In those days, oil was delivered in big trucks with tanks filled with the black substance. My relatives would park their truck in front of each home, then hook up their hose to the oil tank beneath the ground. Natural gas was not even a thought at that time.

The Finkels were religiously minded, starting and supporting temples. My grandfather, the baby of the family, was already well-established as a purveyor of butter and eggs when he arrived in the United States from Galicia, one of the many countries in eastern Europe that have disappeared. Galicia was located between modern-day southeastern Poland and western Ukraine. Fleeing rampant anti-Semitism and religious persecution, Jews across eastern Europe were emigrating to safer lands at the turn of the century. Arriving in the United States around the 1920s, Michael quickly learned the Finkel name was well respected throughout Union County, New Jersey, due to his family's philanthropy and wide range of growing businesses. While Michael never attained the wealth of the rest of his brothers, he always had enough money for whatever he needed.

Among my cousins was the Pulitzer Prize winning author Philip Roth, born a few years after my father. Philip's mother, Bess, was my father's first cousin, and she was a Finkel. Philip looked so much like my father that watching him age was a gift, permitting me to imagine how my father would have looked had he not died so young. In fact, when Philip died, I mourned my father all over again, having now lost the ability to see Philip in photos and on television during one of his rare interviews. Bruce and I watched with pride the HBO production of *The Plot Against America* a few years ago, high-fiving each other each time Bess Finkel's name was spoken. To this day, the Finkel name is still well respected in Elizabeth, New Jersey.

My grandmother was apparently a woman who demanded her way. She was domineering, bombastic, and generally difficult. My grandfather was quiet and resigned. She was in charge of everything.

Grandma Minnie's need to have my father remain a baby as long as possible was obsessive; he was to replace the son she had lost. She refused to toilet train my father, instead fashioning diapers from large swatches of cloth to cover his maturing bottom. Causing Minnie even more anxiety, my father had rheumatic heart disease, which nearly killed him as a child. She slept next to him the first decade of his life, ostensibly to protect him.

As he grew up, my father stuttered on certain letters and words, and he used alternatives to avoid those culprits. He could not say the letter *F* without repeating it countless times. (When he turned forty-four and forty-five, he really struggled.) Studying speech pathology in college, I learned one of the hypotheses for this disorder was that left-handed people who were trained to use their right hand instead of their natural neurological dominance were more likely to stutter. If that is the case, my father was a statistic, sharing he was "changed" as a baby from using his left to his right hand. His handwriting was a work of art, and I imagine it was compensatory to flourish letters, as difficult as it might have been.

Still, my father survived his childhood and became a young man with a charming sense of humor and a mellow crooning voice that would make many become teary. His friendships were plentiful, and his Thomas Jefferson High School yearbook photo stated, "Good humor is always an asset." How ironic—while his good humor was an asset to our family, his dark moods were like currents of electricity charging through our entire house.

My father was also a brilliant mathematician, receiving a scholarship to Columbia University in New York upon his graduation from high school in Elizabeth. But the world had other plans for my father's future. Pearl Harbor was bombed a month before my father's eighteenth birthday, and the United States entered World War II. The marines, looking for "a few good men," recruited heavily in Elizabeth, New Jersey. Like so many of his friends, my father saw this opportunity as his future. Before he could attend Columbia, my father became a marine.

The marines trained my young father to become a bombardier. His base was on Guadalcanal, the principal island in the southwestern Pacific Ocean. From there, day in and day out, he crouched into the back of tin-can bombers. He got close enough to the Japanese enemy that he could see their young faces as they shot the bombers down in flames. Returning to base each evening, the fliers tallied their casualties. I assume each day felt pretty much like the one before, and the daily dogfights became routine. What a burden that young company must have carried.

My father never spoke of those moments and the scars they left. I can only imagine the emotional damage he suffered in the war before our society understood the impact of PTSD. Still, while I assume that my father, like so many others, must have experienced the depression and anxiety of PTSD after the war, I believe it is also important to mention that I have been told he, like the other men in his family, had leanings in that direction even before. As we know, these tendencies certainly continued for the rest of his life.

An interesting story bears out this truth. One day when Allison was nine or ten, I arrived early to pick her up from gymnastics class, and with my extra time, I ran to a supermarket near the gym. I was wandering the aisles when I noticed a stunning woman, older than I, dressed in an eye-catchingly unique cape and skirt ensemble. Being a fashion hound, I was excited to chat with her; I loved her look and wanted to know more about her.

When we wound up at the same checkout line, I turned to her and stated, "You look stunning!" She graciously offered me her hand and introduced herself—her last name was Finkel. Wide-eyed, I told her that was my maiden name, and when she asked which Finkel my father was, I told her he had died many years before.

"Was he a depressed man?" she asked.

Now my eyes grew even wider. "Yes, yes, he was, and he was also plagued with periods of great energy and grandiosity."

"He had to be part of my husband's family. The men all suffer from the same hell."

I have never forgotten her words, even all these years later. Thanks to that mental disorder, the women in our family must have all suffered from the same hell! I was filled with gratitude that day because our experience was someone else's as well. Different from "misery loving company" this realization told me that my father's genetics were in charge of his control over his behavior, like his family. This stunning, well-dressed woman, purchasing her dinner that evening as I was doing the same, gave me a gift—that of belonging. As sad as it was, there were others who knew how it felt to share this pathology. It had been so lonely, living with a man half dead at times and high above the clouds at others. It wasn't until his shiva that a few of his cousins shared their awareness of my father's struggles. There was no relief knowing that what my family had seen all of our lives was true pathology. My sisters and I had already borne the weight of his behaviors to such an extent that we could have testified in a court of law about what life with an untreated sufferer was like.

Growing up, I constantly looked for ways to make my father happy, to make him smile, to make his eyes shine, as I knew they could. Perhaps watching young men die, life leaving their eyes, had made him numb. Maybe he was even numb to his sadism as his lemons burned my sun-blistered knuckles and he watched my adoring eyes well with the tears I was determined not to let flow. What a game we played, but he was always the victor, and I the victim. I have hated seeing myself as a victim, as I was throughout my childhood and young adulthood. As an adult, I have worked very hard to never look at myself that way again. It was too easy to throw in the towel and ask myself, *What do you expect?* Look at those who mentored me. I learned at their knee. But the inner fight I had was to make things better, to not lay down my sword but find a way to carry it with the best intentions. Strength to fight another day took on different meanings with each challenge, but I have always felt that more was expected of me than of others. And I have salved my wounds by going the extra mile to prove myself worthy.

A talented clarinetist and crooner, during his years in the military, my father entertained the troops at night, flushing the memory of death. Tall, thin, and glowing with charisma, his smiling persona must have belied the turmoil within. I often wonder if he was singing to a woman he hoped to meet, an imaginary woman who would fill his heart with love upon his return from the battles he faced ahead.

Twice my father was called back from the South Pacific to New Jersey to bury a parent. First, his beloved mother died of a stroke, and then his father's vacant eyes began to cause my father great concern. My father was right to be concerned; during the six months following my grandmother's death, my grandfather relieved the sadness of his broken heart in the only way he knew—he ingested a little iodine, a few drops at a time, to poison himself. As I grew up, I thought dying of a broken heart, which was how my father described it, was romantic. It wasn't until after my own father's death that I discovered from his friends, who shared the truth, what he had really meant by the term. Suicide. Amid the war, my father was now alone.

After the war, when servicemen and women returned to their sweethearts, my father returned only to his sister, her husband Paul, and their new baby, Ira. My father struggled terribly to bear his loneliness and the trauma of the war, along with the boulder he carried on his back. The boulder was his cycle of periodic, overwhelming depression followed by intense surges of energy. If he had lived until today, he would have finally been diagnosed with and treated for bipolar disorder. But back then his illness went unrecognized and untreated.

Yet like so many soldiers of his generation, my father returned to a life that had changed dramatically. His country was newly energized and recharged, and he was now a man of twenty-three years, a man who wanted a family of his own.

Immediately after the war, the USO hosted numerous dances and events to help the country's discharged armed forces build social lives. My father always volunteered to perform, and one night, while playing the clarinet on the bandstand in Newark, he saw my beautiful mother, age twenty-two, across the room. In my fantasy, my parents' eyes magically found each other. Her deep-green eyes beckoned to his; she radiated sadness, which made him feel important. Leaving the bandstand, my father asked my mother to dance. Their connection was instantaneous.

That is my memory of the story my mother told us. However, my sister Michele remembers it differently. Her memory is this: Both of my parents were at a Y dance (at the YMHA or Young Men's Hebrew Association) when my father saw my mother exiting the ladies' room and introduced himself. "I am Hy Finkel, and I am going to marry you," he allegedly told her. Either way, my parents' life together began as a magical tale. Coincidentally, Michele met her husband Ira at a Y dance, and I met Bruce at a similar dance as well.

Within a few days, my parents were discussing their future. My mother shared with my sisters and I that she felt like a princess, rescued by her prince. In a matter of eight weeks, they were married. My mother wore a borrowed mint-green dress and a smile that showed she had been saved. Or so she hoped.

My father chose California for them to begin their marriage. Having been debriefed in Monterey for a few weeks upon reentering the United States after the war, he already loved the weather and was eager to bring his bride there. My mother was more than willing to join him, even though this meant moving far from her family.

Soon after my parents exchanged vows, they stepped into my father's new Dodge. Their few suitcases, filled with hopes and dreams, rested in the trunk. When night arrived, they found a motel along the highway and consummated their marriage. Their coupling, my mother told me when I was a preteen, was tender and special, full of excitement and plans for their future. My mother was now certain she had found her prince. All her life, my mother was proud of the fact that she was a virgin on her wedding night and held this as an accomplishment that all of her daughters should achieve. She even continued calling herself throughout her life, for some reason we never understood, a virgin, despite having three daughters.

Awakening early the morning after her wedding night, my mother bathed and dressed for another day of travel. She reached out to awaken her sleeping husband, but he did not stir. He had sunk into the deepest sleep she had ever seen. When she pushed harder and called him to wake up, he yelled at her to leave him alone. Then he turned his back to her and continued sleeping.

After breakfast alone, my mother returned to the dark motel room where her new husband was still asleep. "Please get up, Hy. We have to get on the road," she pleaded. As he slept for a full twenty-four hours, my mother began to panic. She was miles from a home to which she had no desire to return, and her marriage already seemed to be unraveling. She was devastated.

But the next morning, my father awakened with a smile and danced her around the room. He was joyful as they continued on their way to their new life in California. He had purchased a dry-cleaning business with his inheritance and was excited by the prospect of arriving. Lily Ann French Cleaners represented their ticket to everything they wanted. They would both work there, she in the shop, and he on the road picking up and delivering cleaning. He referred to himself as a "CPA": Cleanings, Pressings, and Alterations. In his mind, he had found the winning formula, and he was already certain their business would be a success.

When I was a little girl, my mother used to tell me there was a prince growing up across the ocean in a country called England. His name was Prince Charles, and he had been born about a month before I was. She told me I would meet and marry him and live happily ever after. What a fairy tale, particularly poignant because of the tragedy of Diana. I think my mother needed to believe in magical thinking because of the horrific reality of her childhood. These stories were entertaining, but I was less imbued with fantasy as a child.

Yet ironically, the night I met Bruce at a B'nai B'rith Girls/American Zionist Association dance, when I was almost fifteen years old, I told my mother about him, and she told me, "That's the boy you are going to marry." Two weeks later, his father picked us up from a high school dance where I was Bruce's date, and he told Bruce the same thing.

I am amazed that having grown up with a couple who were so cruel and vicious to each other, I still fell in love (okay, first in "like," maybe in lust, and then in love) so easily. Fortunately, I never thought about mirroring my parents' marriage in any way. That is a true blessing, or I would have lost the most stable and loving gift I have.

CHAPTER FOUR
LITTLE GIRL LOST: MY MOTHER

My mother was the eldest of five children. According to family lore, she was possibly the love child of my grandmother Gittel and the love of her life, Yacob, a young man who died before my mother was born. My mother may have had more than a father-daughter relationship with the man she thought was her father, my grandfather Max. Would that be considered sexual abuse and incest? Yes, it would be.

I have often wondered: If she were sexually abused as a child, wouldn't that trauma have splintered her consciousness and scarred her emotionally for the rest of her life? My mother described my grandfather climbing into her crib, and then, when she was older, climbing into her bed. She told me these nightly visits assuaged her father's anxiety, that listening to her breathe made him feel secure, lulling him to sleep. But what did these nightly visits do to her? I have read that when any emotion becomes unmanageable, psychosis can occur. My mother never believed that our pain came close to her own, never believed our issues deserved consideration, because hers were so much worse. She let us know that over and over again. And if these stories are true, she was actually right.

My mother never recovered from her father's death, which occurred when she was fourteen. All of our lives, until our own father's death, she told my sisters and me that her mother had only lost her husband, but she had lost her father. Then when we lost our father, our mother told us that we had only lost our father, but she had lost her husband. Regardless of the way she looked at it, she believed that she was suffering more—more than her mother had, more than we were. Her father's death also forced my mother to leave school after eighth grade to work. Although this was not unusual during the years of the Great Depression, my mother carried a great deal of shame about this loss of her education. My father belittled her lack of education as well. Yet she had a social intelligence that was exceptionally high. People were attracted to her smile, her beauty, and her interest in them. Her social dexterity was her superpower; it enabled her to charm our teachers, shoplift from stores, and even work her way into the homes of the unsuspecting mothers of newborns to sell them baby pictures while posing as a visiting nurse to gain their trust.

She had four siblings: two sisters and two brothers. As the eldest, she took on enormous responsibilities: preparing meals, cleaning, doing laundry, and caring for her family while her mother cleaned houses and ironed for the neighborhood. Even when my grandfather was alive, my mother's family had nothing. As he gambled away everything they earned, my grandmother became filled with hatred and rage. Their fights were enormous, and Gittel frequently threatened to throw her ne'er-do-well husband out. Some of these stories my mother shared with my sisters and me, but more often than not, my mother saw Max as a god. We learned more about the negative sides of her family life from Gittel and our other relatives.

After Max's death, my grandmother and mother did whatever they could to provide for my mother's four younger siblings. They scrubbed floors, ironed clothes, and washed windows. They waited on government food lines for bread, milk, cheese, and potatoes, then rushed home to care for the younger children, who ranged in age from six to thirteen. Both my grandmother and my mother were constantly worried and exhausted. My beleaguered mother was deprived of her youth. Rats inhabited her home, and when I was a child, she would share with me stories of them climbing her legs at night. Nightmares of them breaking the skin awakened her to the reality of them doing just that. The cacophony of squealing and scratching became her nightly lullaby.

She and my grandmother had a tempestuous relationship, both needing each other more than they would admit. The thread of their lives wove through decades of anger and disappointment. Perhaps my grandmother withheld love from my mother because she represented a painful reminder of the man Gittel had fallen in love with and lost—Yacob died of typhus on the ship that was carrying them from Poland toward a new life together in the United States. Or perhaps my mother's belief that she wasn't loved stemmed from her anger as she remembered her father coming to her crib and then to her bed to be satisfied. Perhaps my mother blamed my grandmother for Max's abuse since Gittel had withheld love from him after giving birth to five children. Or perhaps my mother's mental illness, her borderline personality disorder, made it impossible for her to ever feel loved or show love. Whatever the cause of the terrible discord between my mother and her mother, it was all my sisters and I knew, all we heard.

"You are not loved by your only living grandparent," my mother frequently reminded us, just as she reminded us that she was not loved by her only living parent. Throughout our lives, over and over again, my mother told us we were nothing to Grandma Gittel, that she only had love for her twelve other grandchildren.

At my grandmother's funeral, I heard my dozen first cousins share loving memories of how she had cared for them, nurtured them, and prepared their favorite foods. They were mourning a woman with whom I felt so little connection. As time passed, I recognized how poisoned my sisters and I had been by my mother. My mother had felt less than others, she told us we were less than others, and so we felt less than others. I can't, however, help but wonder how different our lives could have been if we had had any adult consistently show us love and affection, acceptance and adoration, direction and stability.

Today I realize how important a mother's sense of self-worth truly is; it not only shapes her identity but also impacts the development of her children. Had my mother felt worthy of her mother's love, my sisters and I would have also felt worthy of Gittel's love. Instead, speaking for myself, I grew up feeling that my grandmother had no affection for me. *Why would she love me?* I wondered. Additionally, the enigmatic fact that she never learned to speak English, despite living in this country for over seventy years, created a further obstacle to our getting to know each other. Today as a mother, I tell my daughters, their husbands, and our grandchildren that I love them every time I see them or speak with them. I want there to be no question of how much I love them so they never wonder if they are lovable.

During World War II, before meeting my father, my seventeen-year-old mother became a riveter in a munitions factory in Newark to replace the men who had gone to war. I imagine she must have met many other women working to save our country, and just as I am proud of my father's service, I am equally proud of hers. I can only assume that my mother also felt pride in her ability to contribute to the war effort, but those were different times. I don't believe women were as acknowledged or celebrated for their work as they should have been. It seems immediately after the war, there was a return to a patriarchal society, which barely recognized the support women like my mother had provided to our country.

When the war ended, my mother was, like my father, ready to begin a new life. That life began the night she and a friend dressed in their best clothes, my mother in a brown sheath with a thick belt enhancing her tiny waist. My mother's hair was styled and her lipstick perfectly applied. I imagine she wore the very popular Victory Red by Elizabeth Arden, an homage to the times, creating the perfect hunter's bow on her mouth. She must have looked stunning.

In my fantasy, as my mother was swaying to the music from the bandstand, she locked eyes with the clarinetist. He was tall and thin with thick, shiny black hair. Moving closer, as if in a trance, she fulfilled her need to see the color of his eyes. They were the darkest brown-black she had ever seen. She felt herself completely taken by this man's presence, and as he put down his clarinet and began to sing in the sweetest voice, she quickly fell for him. Leaving the bandstand, he jumped the few steps down to the dance floor. He landed near her and asked her for a dance.

In either version of their story, my sister Michele's or mine, that dance changed her life. He was her ticket out of the life she knew. Leaving her family would be difficult, but the Little Girl Lost thought she had found what she craved: love, security, fulfillment. I reiterate these stories, either true or fantasy, because I want to believe, even for a few brief moments, that my mother was truly about to find happiness, and my father was as well. But alas, this isn't a fairytale. Their hopes for a better future didn't last long.

CHAPTER FIVE
MY GRANDMOTHER: THE BEGINNING OF INTERGENERATIONAL TRAUMA

There is a very good possibility that Gittel arrived in this country with a secret—my mother growing in her womb. At seventeen years old, Gittel was in love. Yacob was a carpenter in the Polish shtetl where he and Gittel dreamed of living together and sharing their love. My grandmother was beautiful: petite, fair skinned, and blue eyed with golden-blonde hair she wore in a thick braid. She had high cheekbones and a small nose. Her tiny waist and large breasts were enhanced by the tight corset she laced up each day, holding her breath in order to appear even narrower. She worked in the shtetl cleaning homes, ironing, and hand sewing, saving every penny she earned. She was an observant Jew, never mixing milk with meat, or eating restricted foods, or even touching them. She had an extremely close relationship with her mother, my great-grandmother Tsippa, who I have been told was a loving and caring woman. Every week the two women prepared for Shabbos together, cleaning the house, picking feathers off the chicken, preparing soup, and braiding the challah for dinner. Then, covering their eyes, their heads covered, they lit the candles. My grandmother had a large family of siblings, many of whom had already immigrated to the United States by the time she was a teenager, and they promised to send money for my grandmother to sail to New Jersey as well. She knew her home in the United States would reflect her devotion to tradition, and she would raise her children to follow her beliefs.

Gittel and Yacob wanted more than anything to go to the United States, marry, and start their family. When Yacob looked at her, he could think of nothing else but his desire to give her everything she wanted in life, and more. When he held her, his desire led him to imagine how it would feel to have her alone, all to himself, just his body and hers. He knew he could support her; he would earn a good salary honing wood and crafting it in whatever image his patrons wanted. He was good at his craft, a carpenter who could create almost anything. He would be a loving and devoted husband, and he and Gittel would have a good life in the new country—of this, he was certain.

Leaving her mother, Tsippa, would be difficult, but Gittel knew her mother would be making the voyage in a few months, when more money could be sent for her passage. As Gittel waited for notice, her siblings booked a ticket for her on a large ship, ready to sail within a few days. Gittel was bereft when she told Yacob she would be leaving, but he thrilled her by announcing that he too had saved money to travel to America.

It was more obvious than ever that Yacob was in love with her and as committed to her as she was to him. They were floating on their dreams and expectations. They had heard so much about the opportunities in the United States for a couple willing to work hard, save their money, and create their future.

The day Gittel and Yacob boarded the ship and left the port in Poland, my grandmother had only a carpetbag made of scraps of multicolor fabrics she had sewn together, filled with her few dresses, a corset, underwear, a nightgown, and slippers. Yacob hoisted her luggage onto the ship along with his own. They settled in for what would be a harrowing crossing. They were elated, however, to have and hold each other, looking ahead to their new life across the sea.

Sadly, a few days into their lengthy trip, both Yacob and Gittel contracted typhus and fell into comas. My grandmother awoke; Yacob did not. Upon hearing he had perished, she wailed and wailed, certain her life was over. In truth, the life she had envisioned with Yacob, loving and feeling cherished, had vanished forever.

Over the years, my grandmother had one confidant, my cousin, with whom she shared her stories. I have gleaned these events of Gittel's life from my conversations with this cousin, as she learned them in conversations with my grandmother. Admittedly, I do not know if it is true that my grandmother was pregnant with my mother when she immigrated to the United States, but if it is true, I believe this is how Gittel's story continued ....

Gittel arrived at Ellis Island distraught—and possibly pregnant with my mother. Upon seeing her brothers, Louis and Abe, she broke down and sobbed. They decided they would have to make a plan to take care of her. Who was going to financially support this single woman, and possibly her baby too?

The brothers knew Max, a widower who had recently moved to the area. He was a cattle rancher, and meat was an expensive commodity. Hearing that the brothers had a pretty sister who had just arrived from Poland, Max offered them a deal: Gittel would marry him, and he would keep the family well fed. To sweeten the deal, he brought with him a burlap bag filled with multiple cuts of meat wrapped in wax paper and tied in string. The ensuing discussion among the men focused on whether or not Max would be attracted to Gittel. After all, Max knew he held the cards; the deal depended upon his decision. For Louis and Abe, much was at stake, and Max's agreement was imperative. If, in fact, Gittel was pregnant, then Max would need to believe he was the father of the baby. His feelings of ownership were vitally important as he would need to care for Gittel, and her family, for the rest of his life.

Max came to the parlor of the brothers' duplex a few days later, once Gittel had been scrubbed clean from her trip, her long braid undone, washed, and braided again, her best dress pressed after her long journey. Max deemed her acceptable; of course, Gittel had no say in the matter. They were married soon after. So all of my grandmother's dreams shattered.

Not only was her dream of a loving life with Yacob now impossible, but she also found herself joining the numerous women forced into arranged marriages and the trauma that accompanied them. I can only imagine her feelings of alienation, disconnection, and loss of hope.

My grandmother may have had a secret pregnancy, but Max had a huge secret of his own. Two years before Max became Gittel's husband, he had lived and done most of his cattle breeding in an entirely different part of New Jersey, far from where he met Gittel and her family. Central South Jersey was the home of cattle and chicken farmers; there, the soil was rich for growing verdant produce, for farming, and for ranching. Max and his wife Essie had a small bungalow on a farm where Max was responsible for maintaining the property for the owner. It should have been a profitable situation for Max, but he had a problem that caused him constant financial instability.

Max regularly met a group of men who gathered to gamble at whatever games enticed them, and he was always welcome. He would puff out his chest and show off the money in his pocket, constantly ready to throw his earnings into whatever pot might bring him luck. Gambling was his pleasure—or his addiction. Winning was rarely the result.

When Essie gave birth to a beautiful baby, Sophie, Max adored her. She had dazzling blonde curls and dark-blue eyes. He couldn't get enough of her nuzzling into his neck when he held her. His love for her was insatiable, as was his lust for Essie. But Essie grew punishing when he didn't bring home the weekly pay she knew he had earned. Meanwhile, Max's demands were harsh and cruel, his desires unloving and only self-satisfying. There was little love between Max and Essie, and both grew filled with anger.

Essie knew where Max's money was going, and now that they had a baby, she was unable to tolerate his behavior. She rejected him repeatedly, and he retaliated by demanding more from her sexually, domineering her with his perceived power as the breadwinner, and gambling away whatever money he earned. One day, after Max had loaded his truck and left for the day, Essie put water into the tea kettle on the old stove and waited for it to boil. She took a tea ball from the pantry and poured the boiling water over the tea. While her cup of tea steeped, she took a rubber enema bag and filled it with the remaining contents of the tea kettle. Capping the bag with the nozzle, she placed Sophie on the kitchen table, pushed the hose into her tiny rectum, and sent the boiling water through her little body. Sophie's screams only lasted a short while, and then Essie drank her tea. When Max returned and opened the door to the bungalow, he saw his beautiful Sophie lying dead on the table, stiff and startled, her eyes open like a doll's.

Falling to his knees in horror, Max was unable to conceive that his precious Sophie could actually be dead. Max looked around the room and screamed for Essie. She waltzed into the room wearing her prettiest dress, her face painted as if she were ready to attend a dance. She stared at him as if she were the winner at one of his gambling tables. She felt neither remorse for her actions nor pity for Sophie and Max. The only sorrow Essie felt was for herself. Her ultimate revenge for all the money he had lost—and for his brazen taking of her whenever he wanted—had cost her Sophie, but Essie was young, she told herself, and would have more children.

Max, enraged, contemplated killing Essie with one of his butchering tools but had no stomach for murder. Instead, he planned a new life in North Jersey as a widower, pretending his wife was dead and believing his secret was quite safe. In his mind, babies died all the time, so no one would be the wiser about Sophie. He would not report Essie; how could he ever face people again if he had to acknowledge being married to a woman who had murdered their child to punish him? No, it was better this way. He was gone, people assuming he had left unable to cope with the death of his child, and whatever else they thought of him didn't matter. He needed to be free of the memory of that marriage, that loss.

Years later, while talking with another rancher, Max learned that Essie had taken her own life, drinking a cocktail of cleaning fluids. Like Essie after Sophie's death, Max felt neither remorse for his behavior nor pity for his spouse. Essie's death meant, for certain, his secret would remain safe. It died with Essie and was the end of that part of his life. However, somehow my grandmother must have learned the story since she shared it with my cousin, who shared it with me. My mother never told me the real story about her father's life, and I have to believe she knew, if my cousin knew. My mother never hesitated, as far as I knew, to extol stories of misery visited upon her and her family, so it is suspect why she never shared this horrendous one with me or my sisters. Was there duplicity in my mother's decision to withhold the truth about Max, in her wanting to believe, or have our family believe, only the best of her father in order to blame her mother for what she perceived as a lack of love?

My cousin also told me about more members of our extended family who had committed incest, abuse, and other acts of violence. This knowledge reinforced for me that every human behavior we view as part of today's world has existed for generations and generations. I believe in the saying: "Nothing is new under the sun!"

Leaving Essie in the past, Max felt relieved, ready, and grateful for a new start with a young wife who would satisfy his every need. Meeting Gittel's brothers, Louis and Abraham, felt fortuitous. The men discussed what each would bring to the arrangement, a fairly simple one: Max would provide for the family, and Gittel would provide for Max.

Within eight years, my grandmother had five children: three daughters and two sons. Her rapidly growing family meant never-ending demands on her, and her misery was palpable. Regardless of how long her days were, there was always more to do. And Max was not interested in giving up his passion for gambling. The duplex Max was able to afford was on a street in Irvington, close to Gittel's sister Eva and her family. Eva and her husband, Willy, who had come to this country years before her brothers, owned a delicatessen, where my grandmother took food as payment for the cleaning and ironing she did at their home. Well aware that she was the poor relative, Gittel was grateful for the opportunity to provide food for her family. Max rarely managed to bring home or hold on to much money but continued to expect Gittel to meet his every need. After five children, Gittel was done with sex. She kept a knife under her pillow, and when Max came to her, she let the gleaming steel speak for itself. Max retreated.

The duplex had an alcove where my mother slept to escape the maturing eyes of Jacob, her younger brother by thirteen months. This alcove was a small space, but it offered privacy, a privacy that beckoned to Max. The abuse started with his climbing into my mother's crib when she was a baby, then into her bed as she grew. He stroked and caressed her sleeping body. As she got older, my mother would imagine she was dreaming, but when she awoke, she responded to his touch lovingly, adoringly. These reactions were compelling to a man who felt sexually unsatisfied and needed to dominate others in order to feel powerful. As time passed, my mother grew more eager for his touch.

My mother never revealed to Gittel the feelings she had for her father, but she shared these stories with me. She assured me she had been happy when her father felt secure in her bed, happy when he was able to sleep beside her. The funny thing is that until I started writing my memoir, it had never occurred to me that there may have been sexual relations involved in their relationship. Perhaps the truth was the way my mother presented it. Or perhaps the abuse she endured was so overwhelming for her that she had to normalize it in order to live with it.

If Gittel had any idea how Max was satisfying his lust, she never spoke of it. She was relieved to have nothing to do with the man who had caused her so much misery. He remained demanding and callous, gambling away their money, and Gittel never felt a moment of love for him. She sneered when her daughters showed him affection, glaring at Max and her daughters.

When he was forty-six years old, Max was kicked by a bull in the abdomen while attempting to wrestle the beast into his pen. Lying on the ground, Max vomited blood and screamed ungodly sounds in his agony. Nothing could soothe him, although his children rushed to his side. Gittel stood away, watching from afar, since she felt nothing for him as he suffered. Soon thereafter, while sleeping in the same bed where he had fathered his children, Max passed away. Gittel never cried. All she could remember was the difference between the way he took her, hard and quick, and the soft and loving way she and Yacob had made love. There would never be another man in her life, of that she was certain. She had no need for a man to waste her family's money, make demands on her, or expect her to love him. That need had died years ago.

Nevertheless, Gittel wailed at Max's funeral and threw herself onto the grass beside the open pit where his body would be laid. Her siblings assumed that her wailing reflected her love and adoration for her dead husband, but nothing could have been further from reality. Gittel knew that her life, as poor as it had been when Max was alive, would now be worse, and that frightened her beyond measure.

When my grandfather died, leaving bills, gambling debts, and no money, the eldest child, my mother, left school to stand on line for bread, milk, eggs, and other foods the family needed. When he graduated from high school, the second eldest, Jacob, got a job in a factory in the next town, but my mother's family still lived hand to mouth each day. Gittel's brothers and their families had benefited from the arrangement they had made with Max, but upon his death, they felt no responsibility for his widow and her young children. So Gittel cleaned houses, ironed, and mended clothing for others before doing the same for her own children.

As the years passed and each child married and created their own families, my grandmother lived the life of a nomad. Each of her five children took her into their home for a predetermined length of time. My mother was the child who made Gittel's life one of anguish. Regardless of where my grandmother was living, my mother would telephone her each morning and scream about how unloved she felt. Not only would she cry that she felt unloved, my mother would also cry that my grandmother did not love her grandchildren either. As I have mentioned, my sisters and I grew familiar with the constant message that we were not treasured by anyone. My mother's incessant fighting with my grandmother also created chaos for my mother's siblings, who had to cope with my grandmother's rage at being attacked each morning. Sadly, my mother's attacks remained unrelenting until my grandmother was moved to a nursing facility.

I do not know why my grandmother never learned to speak English throughout all of her years in the United States. Perhaps it was because she had five children within eight years, or perhaps it was because her five children spoke for her and navigated her life to the extent that she didn't have to learn English. Either way, as she grew older, not speaking English made my grandmother even more of a prisoner in this country. She truly was a captive—first by Max, then five needy children, no money or source of income other than low-paying jobs to support them, and then the inability, or lack of desire, to speak the language of the country that had been her home for more than seventy years. Her five children gave her fifteen grandchildren, but in her eighties, her only pleasure was watching soap operas and drinking tea with a sour ball in her jaw as she drank.

Near the end of her life, my grandmother was brought to a nursing facility that her children felt affordable when split among the five of them. There she was shunned. Her inability to speak English separated her from the other residents, and they looked down on her lack of education. Furthermore, the staff believed her to be ignorant and had no patience when she spoke to them in her mixture of Yiddish and the few English words she knew.

One morning, when Gittel was dressing, an aide brought her a pair of shoes, clearly too large for her tiny feet. She began to cry, "*Nish mi shichela*s." (Not my shoes.) She cried it over and over again, getting louder each time. The aide ignored her screams. Annoyed it was her turn to assist Gittel, the aide distractedly placed Gittel's walker in front of the oversized shoes. When Gittel, wearing the poorly fitting shoes, tried to take a step, she tripped over the walker, hitting her face and breaking her nose and cheekbone. The aide quickly pulled the walker away, causing my grandmother to hit the floor with such force that she fractured her pelvis and hip as well. These injuries proved to be too much for Gittel; she was as broken as her heart had been for decades.

Dying, Gittel called for my mother to come to her, which she did. I was there with my mother, and I stood off to the side as she leaned over my grandmother, her tiny face bruised from the fall, her eyes wet with tears. The nurse told us that she had been screaming for my mother for the longest time. It was truly heartbreaking to see my grandmother so irreparably hurt.

Whispering in my mother's ear in her native Yiddish, I imagine my grandmother said that it was always her belief that Lillian's father, the man she had loved her entire life, had been sweet and kind. Perhaps Yacob came alive again, to my mother, as my grandmother shared the story of herself as a young woman, her golden braid falling onto her lover's chest.

But that is the romantic in me. According to my mother, my grandmother had exhausted herself from screaming for her all morning, and as she bent down and whispered, "I am here, Mama," my grandmother grabbed my mother's hand and took her last breath.

CHAPTER SIX
THE BLUE BABY SCALE

Lily Ann French Cleaners in Burbank, California, was the new beginning both of my parents wanted.

Following the deaths of his parents within six months of each other, my father had inherited money. Aside from purchasing a new Dodge for his cross-country trip with my mother from New Jersey to California, he saved his money for the start of their new business. His enthusiasm was contagious, exciting my mother as well. As I have mentioned, he laughingly referred to himself as a "CPA": Cleanings, Pressings, and Alterations.

Although that was his moniker, he had little to do with the actual cleaning, pressing, or alteration of any clothing. While my mother did the cleaning and managed the shop, he traveled the tree-lined streets of Los Angeles's wealthy neighborhoods: Hollywood, Beverly Hills, and Hancock Park. He preferred working outside the shop, as he had never thought past his initial excitement at owning a business. He had never considered the responsibilities he and his wife now shared. He found these newfound responsibilities depressing. Conversely, my mother was delighted whenever she saw the opportunity to earn a dollar, a dollar she had never had before.

My father's pickup route was impressive, including the homes of Danny Thomas, Nat King Cole, Sophie Tucker, Dean Martin, Jerry Lewis, and Sammy Davis Jr. Their mansions and estates covered twisting roads. My father drove the long circular driveways that meandered like syrup on waffles and entered the back doors into the kitchens of the rich and famous. He loved chatting with the women and men who serviced the lives of the wealthy. They recognized another struggling man, even though he was White, and in most cases, they were Black and Brown. He was ebullient and entertaining, telling jokes and dancing the women around the kitchens where they prepared and cooked celebrities' food. Eager to hear the gossip in the neighborhood, he rarely refused a cup of coffee and a piece of freshly baked pie before heading to another enormous kitchen.

So all of those celebrities became part of my quilt of memories of that era. As my father regaled me over and over again with his stories of each interaction, I felt I had been there with him, even before I was born. One of the stories he shared several times with me, a tragic one, was at the Hancock Park home of Nat King Cole in 1948. He was delivering clothes, carrying the plastic-covered suits and dresses, the day the "King's" dog was found poisoned, just days after the letter N was burned onto the lawn. My father wept that day and each time he told me the story. My heart broke even as he sat in his cushioned chair, his eyes miles away, and I can't help but wonder what he would make of the hatred that still exists today.

Until my father's death, when my mother threw out his autograph book along with his other possessions, I used to love to open that book and read the names of the stars, not only because they were so famous but also because I believed they had regarded my father well as they signed their names. I was so proud of him, of the way he glowed when describing each and every interaction with these well-known, well-respected entertainers, directors, and movie moguls.

My father's favorite song was "Nature Boy," by the Nat King Cole Trio. He sang it to me wistfully, soulfully, sadly, breaking my heart each and every time. The words spoke to me, the story of a strange, sad-eyed, perhaps enchanted boy who traveled the world speaking of mysteries, imaginings, and thoughts he alone, in his wisdom, understood. The ending, which my father slowly exhaled a few times, told me that loving and being loved in return are the greatest things one can ever learn.

(Not long ago, while watching the Broadway version of *Moulin Rouge!* which featured the song, I grabbed Bruce's arm and dug my nails in, shaking with pathos. I saw my father as the young man he had been when he died, dark hair still full and shiny, black cherry eyes glowing, speaking to me from another universe. He was telling me what he had always told me in this song: Loving and being loved in return are the greatest things one can ever learn. Pathetically, he was never able to show he loved us—how sad that must have been for him. It was for us. And most painful to me, did he know I loved him?)

I share this poignant song with you because there were times when melancholy crossed my father's face, when I thought of Nat King Cole, Sophie Tucker, Dean Martin, and the many other people with stature, and knew my father felt "less than," no longer the owner of Lily Ann French Cleaners, no longer a "CPA," no longer back in his beloved California. I would ask him, as a distraction, to sing "Nature Boy," which he usually did, and the haunting melody filled the room. He held my trembling heart in his hands. Tears well in my eyes even as I write this, decades and decades later. Perhaps there is still a part of me that withers as he did, or perhaps there is a part of me that saw him as wandering the earth, for the short time he was here, to share a message of love, even if he had such a difficult time showing it.

Returning to the dry-cleaning shop in downtown Burbank brought out the worst in my father. By the time he approached the back door, he was already angry and anxious. Carrying the big canvas sacks of others' dirty clothes made him feel trivialized and miserable. The difference between him and those who had too much grew enormous in his eyes, and he felt trapped by my mother with her pregnant belly and her demands. Her feet were swollen, her belly got in the way of hanging the clothes, and she was always tired.

My father's one coping skill was to escape to his bed, for one day or several. But before he could retreat to sleep, he had to start a fight with my mother so he had reason to take shelter in what she referred to as his crib. The baby she was carrying, which was me, was a perfect target. As her belly grew, so did his anger. She tried to lose the baby, throwing herself down the stairs, and that made him angry as well. Then he would accuse her of thinking he was a monster who wanted her to terminate his child. Ultimately, my mother tried to abort all three of her children. My father wanted, then didn't want, then wanted a child, and my mother was probably equally confused by her feelings about having us.

When my father awakened from his stupor, a few days or a week later, his happiness would radiate like the warmth of the sky. He dressed and found my mother sipping her coffee in the kitchen, her belly pushing through the dress she had borrowed from her sister Shirley. He pulled my mother close enough to him that his aftershave made her, sensitive and pregnant, nearly gag. But she held on to these moments and danced in his arms around the kitchen as he crooned in her ear: *"I love you so, and I love our baby, and life is going to be wonderful,"* and on and on. All the same words she had heard before.

Much more prescient than my father, my mother knew that the expense of hiring someone to manage Lily Ann French Cleaners once I was born would take a huge bite out of the small profit my parents had garnered, and she anticipated the impact that adversity would have on my father's fragile psyche. My father did not recognize the hardships ahead. He was happy when he was happy, and he didn't want anything to make him unhappy. Until the reverse was, sadly, true.

I arrived soon thereafter, close to two years after my parents' arrival in Southern California. My father became doting and energized, jumping in his car to drive his cleaning route to the stars. He couldn't wait to share his news with everyone he met. I looked very much like him, dark hair and pale skin. He was convinced there had been no more beautiful baby ever born.

Housekeepers on my father's cleaning route heard of my birth with joy, and each day they sent little gifts home with him. Some were toys, rattles, and bibs, things to let my father know he was important to the business of caring for the masters of the homes.

Danny Thomas, a well-respected actor, comedian, and singer, had a son, Tony, born two days before me. Everyone in the entertainment world showered Tony with gifts, more than any little boy could need. An extremely generous man, Mr. Thomas told his kitchen staff to give the extras to the "cleaning man." That night, my father returned home with a car full of baby items, including a blue baby scale and myriad blue blankets and clothes enhanced with boats and farm animals. My father felt important, even indispensable, as he and my mother weighed me for the first time, proud of the scale given to them by Danny Thomas.

Yet my mother became overwhelmed by the confusing feelings she experienced after my birth. My father was so enraptured with me that she felt jealous, then became guilt-ridden by her anger at us, as if we were a team from which she was excluded. She knew that at any moment, my father could retreat to his own crib, leaving her with full responsibility for a newborn and a faltering business that, as she had predicted, was spending more money hiring an employee to do her job than she had earned.

The slightest pressure could cause my father to devolve. She had no way of consoling herself, no way of coping. A baby is a gift, she told herself, but one she knew would cost her in the long run. She was angry with herself. She had wanted a baby because my Aunt Shirley in New Jersey had a daughter. My mother fell in love with my cousin Maureen when she visited her, in love with those big eyes and that dark hair. That became her focus. She wanted to be a mother as well. But she already knew my father's patterns. As she contemplated their future, why would she have assumed that more responsibility would change him?

And then, when I was two years old, my mother became pregnant with my middle sister, Michele. The apartment was noisy, filled with yelling, slamming doors, and frequently, my mother crying as she picked me up from my crib. I tried to be a good girl, putting away my toys, grabbing my parents' legs and hugging them. But my mother and father just kept yelling at each other.

"And you are such a bargain?" he would snap back at my mother when they argued. "I saved you from a life of nothing, brought you to California, and so now you think you're so special?"

"I'm pregnant! I take care of our child, the apartment, keep our business running for another day, standing on my swollen feet," my mother screamed. "All you do is sleep and get angry …. I can't take it anymore!"

Her words were accompanied by a pinch and deep dig of her nails to emphasize her disgust at my father. I felt panic rising and ran under the black lacquer coffee table in the living room, my belly twisting and turning. I felt lost and alone while my parents fought, and my refuge under the table offered no protection from their violence.

My only consolation was the imaginary friend my father created, Squeaky the mouse. Meant to protect me, the mouse represented a projection of my father's attention and cost me my mother's ire each time he or I mentioned Squeaky's name. How could I have anything positive of my father when she couldn't? The irony is that Squeaky was a rodent, related to the rodents who assaulted her as she slept as a child, nibbling at her legs, entangling themselves in her hair, squealing all night. My father wanted to torment her and knew just where the chinks in the armor were.

As a young child, I learned to not hope for much, since undoubtedly, one parent or the other would be angry, if not at me then at the other. Any good times were immediately followed by bad, and any bad times were almost immediately followed by even worse times. I remember having a friend named Joanie. We loved each other. We hugged when we saw each other, and our mothers liked each other as well. I could tell because my mother spoke with Joanie's mom in whispers, which indicated to me that they told each other secrets. I wished I could tell Joanie how scared I was when my parents fought, but I did not have the language I needed to share my own secrets. Perhaps I knew that, either way, there was no way for me to change the conflict in our home.

As tension in our small apartment increased, my father became more and more distant. My mother's eighteen-year-old brother, my Uncle Ted, came from New Jersey to live with us in order to attend UCLA free of tuition. I loved having him there. Initially, he and my father bonded as they spent time together. Yet eventually, even that time of hope ended as my parents' violent fights evolved into different forms. Now doors slammed as my parents chased each other to their bedroom instead of fighting in the small living room. The sounds they made echoed throughout the apartment, nevertheless, and I covered my ears and dove under the coffee table, over and over again. With another person in our small apartment and my mother expecting another child, my father became overwhelmed with panic. He could not bear the pressure of his rising responsibilities. Retreating to his bed took more planning, and picking a fight with my mother was more challenging with another adult in the house. Yet my father's needs, which revolved around running away from all of us, still took center stage, so to bed he went, over and over again. He would take off his pants, hang them on the corner of a closet door, and go to bed ... for however long he needed. His bed was a magnet, an obsession, a place for his anger to reside.

Eventually, when I was a bit older than two, my father lost most of his customers, who waited in vain for the pickup and delivery of their clothes. Regardless of how personable he was with customers, there came a time when his excuses no longer worked on them. People needed their dry cleaning, and their housekeepers needed to find others to do pickups and deliveries. Without his routes, my parents' business was on the verge of folding.

"Get off your rear and get to work!" my mother shouted.

"Get away from me with your ugly claws, and don't you dare tell me what to do! I took you from the rats and gave you a home of your own! You have it so bad?" my father retorted. Even my Uncle Ted had to look away, since we both knew what was coming. Back to bed my father went.

CHAPTER SEVEN
A FEAR OF POLICE

I have always had a fear of doing the wrong thing, and to this day, feeling I have done the wrong thing is one of the few challenges that makes me cry. My parents had a "do as I say, not as I do" policy when it came to modeling behavior, and so I became an excellent, overachieving student, following every rule, excelling at doing as they said, not as they did. My parents were both able to play the system for their own benefit, but I watched and worried that the police would take them away from my sisters and me as punishment for breaking the law. Perhaps I felt I would also be punished for my parents' egregious acts.

Whether my hypermoral compass arose from this fear of the police, or from my awareness of my own imprisonment within my family, or from a feeling that my anxiety could help me avoid the consequences of my parents' actions, actions that were beyond my control, that strict compass kept me from enjoying a lot of life. In college, for example, I avoided friends partaking in the drug culture and sexual revolution, freedoms that I felt would lead to punishment. The prospect of getting caught, and I knew I would, kept me on the straight and narrow and, I imagine, made me not much fun! I expected too much from myself and, perhaps, from others. I knew that there were "good girls" and "nice girls" (actually, "bad girls") and that society graded them primarily by their sexual involvements. I was terrified of being sexual, despite loving and longing for Bruce. We had been going out for years when I went to college, and yet, I was so frightened of becoming a bad girl that I pushed him away when our relationship began to progress physically. In retrospect, I suppose I reacted to our growing intimacy as one who has been traumatized reacts when moving beyond her comfort level.

My lifetime of following the rules likely stemmed from my first experience of seeing firsthand the power and presence of the police. I was two years, eight months, and one day old. This day is indelibly inscribed in my mind because it was the day before my sister Michele was born. The heavy pounding on the door awakened me from my curled-up position in my new big-girl bed. (Since my baby sister or brother would need a place to sleep, I no longer slept in the crib.) Tangled in my blue-and-white boat-trimmed blanket, I slowly became alert over the next few minutes as the banging continued and terror filled my heart. Where were my parents? My tiny fists propped open my bedroom door, and I fearfully looked around our small apartment. There was nobody. The pounding continued, growing louder and louder. A man's big, angry voice yelled for my father to open the door. I knew he was calling for my father. I recognized my father's name. So why wasn't he answering?

My father was tall, and as a young child, I felt safe and protected when he was near me. As I grew older, my father became less and less interested in protecting me or my sisters, having lost his sense of responsibility, one I still feel for my married daughters. Yet back then, even when I went to sleep in the dark, if my father was in the apartment, I felt better.

Alone on that morning, I slid to the wall, my fear rising as the banging on the door escalated. Just then, unaware I had pinned myself to the wall, my father appeared and answered the door. The man with the angry voice was a policeman. I recognized the uniform he wore. Why was he here at our home yelling at my father? Seeing me cowering, the policeman said in a kind voice, "Why don't you get your mommy, sweetheart?"

Crying for my mother, I found her lying across her bed with her big belly on one side and her legs shaking on the other. I worried about the baby, and was scared there was something terribly wrong with my mother.

I had always felt the need to protect my mother, even as she never felt the need to protect me, so caught up she was in her misery and self-pity. She started to whimper, and my father came into the bedroom and sent me out of the room. Then I heard my parents yelling at each other loudly and felt my heart beating very fast. I ran into my room, jumped under the blanket, pulled it over my head, and cried. Eventually, I heard the policeman tell my father he had to come with him to the police station.

Fortunately, when I awoke the next morning, my Uncle Teddy was there with me. He told me he had taken my mother to the hospital last night and I now had a new baby sister, Michele. So I was a big sister, and she was coming to live with us in the crib in my room. Uncle Teddy helped me put on the yellow-and-green sweater and tam with the pom-pom that my Aunt Shirley had knitted for me. Standing in the back seat of the car, I felt giddy with excitement as he told me I was going to see my mother and the baby. "Not my father?" I asked.

Sadly, Baby Number Two was born into chaos. My father remained in jail and wouldn't return home for two weeks, his punishment for selling bogus items. He was a train conductor at that time, having lost Lily Ann French Cleaners—a very sad loss since his inheritance from his parents had paid for the business, and now this gift too was gone. In his side hustle selling bogus items on the train, he would approach well-dressed men who appeared flush with money and sell them fake watches and the like. Upon realizing their purchases were fake, most people just threw them away, perhaps not happy to acknowledge their gullibility. But apparently, someone had pressed charges, hence the visit from the policeman. The stress of this experience may have been the catalyst for my mother to enter early labor, which was breech. Perhaps, had my sister been given more time to turn, my mother may have had an easier delivery.

My mother was so angry at my father that her depression and her inability to care for Michele became obvious to me, and I became Michele's mommy. The only thing that would stop Michele from crying was when I crept up into her crib and held her. I rocked her back and forth, telling her I loved her and that I would protect her when Mommy and Daddy yelled at each other. Sometimes when I had to tell my mother it was time to feed Michele, she simply stared straight ahead, responseless. I didn't know what to do. I was two years, eight months, and two days older than Michele—*a baby myself!* But oh, how I loved my baby. Michele became my baby doll. This is a good time to reflect on how the responsibility I felt for Michele—my reason to awaken in the morning, to rub the sleep from my eyes and run to her crib to check on her and love her, the warmth we created as sisters—was at once my everything, yet it set a tone of hyper-responsibility for so many in my life. I worried more about Michele than anyone. I was never able to be a child, always like a runner at the starting line, pumped up to care for her. When she was sick, I was sicker because I couldn't make her well. Ignored by my parents because they were so consumed with their own needs, I grew angry when I felt she needed more from them, that which she didn't receive.

My father returned home, my Uncle Teddy left, and I grew sad and worried. Who would care for us if my father were taken away again? I remained terrified that the police might bang on our door once again. Yet my last memory of California was caring for my perfect gift, the tiny baby whose hair was the color of the lightest wheat and who had hands as small and soft as a doll's. Michele smelled like what I imagined heaven would and brought me joy I had never known possible. All I ever wanted to do was to protect her from life, from our lives, from our parents. How I believed that if I loved her totally, and if I held her tightly, and if I sang to her and stroked her, then she would never know fear or dread or pain. I was, of course, so wrong. But what power could I expect from myself, a child not yet three years old?

"She is your baby," my mother told me, "and you will always take care of her." And I did. Those prophetic words guided my lifelong adoration for my sister, who never really knew whether our parents would be there to care for her. She followed me around, and when she was old enough to speak, she spoke the most important word to me, *sister.* Michele became my very special dependent. Later, I walked her to and from school each day. She knew exactly where to meet me at dismissal. If I was late because our class had detention, I would cry so fiercely that our teacher had to send another adult to meet Michele and bring her to sit in the back of our class. So deep was my sense of responsibility. So fearful was I that we would cease to exist if I did anything wrong, if I was neglectful in any way.

Ironically, years later, when I was suffering from crippling anxiety, falling apart as I left Emerson College, Michele was the only person who could bring calm to my fragile emotions. I would pick her up from high school, and we would drive for hours until my anxiety faded away. Her presence returned me to a time, I believe, when I had value, tied as it was to my role as caregiver, but it made me feel a sense of calm just being near her. Sadly, when she needed me most, when she was losing her only child, our nephew, Adam, who died of leukemia at thirty-nine years old, I was not able to save her from the worst pain in the world. Over the years, I have often felt that I failed to protect her, but surely that was my biggest failure of all.

The next time I came face-to-face with the police, there were a few of them. I was close to five years old, and our family had moved back from California to New Jersey, where we now lived with my aunts, uncles, and cousins in my grandmother's house in Irvington. Our destination for shopping was Chancellor Avenue. My mother would take Michele in the stroller, and I would walk beside her, holding on to my mother with all my might. It wasn't a dangerous walk, but my mother was unsteady on her feet since she preferred not to wear her glasses. The sidewalks were uneven, and she had fallen previously, hitting her head and causing a large egg to appear on her forehead.

Of the several shops on Chancellor Avenue, my mother's favorite was the small department store, Siegel's. I loved walking around inside. Siegel's was bright and filled with everything from lace handkerchiefs to dressy clothing. I admired the mannequins, with their pretty outfits, hats, and handbags, standing beside the tables and racks of women's and children's apparel. But my happiness was always short-lived. I had a job to do, and I knew, even at that young age, that I was doing something wrong.

Upon entering the store, I was to be as cute as possible, smiling and chatting with shoppers and staff and, all the while, watching the stroller, guarding and protecting my sister while my mother switched the price tags on the items she wanted. I was the distraction from her crimes! In those days, long before clothing stores had computers to spit out prices or plastic threads to secure price tags, the tags were attached with straight pins, which were apparently easy enough to switch. Once the deed was done, the management had to honor the lower price, even if they were aware of the discrepancy.

The first time my mother used me on one of her shoplifting expeditions, I was none the wiser. How would I know why my mother had told me to be so gregarious? When we were approached by a man in a suit who told my mother he "thought" she might have picked up a blouse that had been mismarked, my mother simply shrugged and told him she still wanted to purchase the blouse—so she won. I saw the look of happiness in her eyes, but perhaps it was that of victory, small as it was, and she felt deserving of it because she had outsmarted everyone.

But the next time, she was "made"! When we walked into the store, alarm bells must have sounded in the manager's office. They allowed us to "shop" for a while, then as we exited the fitting room where my mother had successfully lifted other garments in the past, putting them on under her own clothes, a policeman took my mother's arm and brought all three of us upstairs to a large office. Several policemen were already waiting for us. My insides were screaming, and my throat was dry. As I recognized that I had become an accomplice to her stealing, I grew even more terrified. Yes, I was only close to five years old, but I still knew our behavior had been wrong. To this day, I wonder how I ignored my moral compass; I am usually so guided by doing the right thing. I suppose the answer is that, as a child, I knew my mother needed me to be her support system. She had nobody else. She was lost, and my job was to help her find herself.

Michele and I were taken out of the office into an area with plastic dining tables and chairs, and machines with snacks in them. Still, I listened to the conversation in the other room as if my life depended upon it—my head pressed to the wall, ear working its hardest to catch glimpses of words—because I truly thought it did. I heard the police tell my mother that she would be arrested if she entered the store again and that she was in danger of losing Michele and me. Then the police told my mother that she would have to go to court to answer these charges, but they were not the kind that sent people to jail ... yet. It was a hearing, but it was serious. At that time, I assumed Michele and I would go to live with one of our aunts or uncles, but thinking about it now, we most probably would have been placed into the foster care system. It is so interesting to me that I never thought we would live with my father.

When Michele and I went to court with my mother, she cried with humiliation. She told the judge that she needed to take these things because my father didn't work and there was no other way for her to clothe her children. My mother's story was heartbreaking. She was ordered to see a social worker named Mrs. Landa for several sessions. As I listened, I wondered how my mother would get there. Would we be traveling on a bus with Michele's stroller? I knew we didn't have a lot of money, and I worried about how we would pay for the bus. So we returned home, my sister in her stroller, and me walking closely alongside my mother in case she began to fall. I suppose one could say she *had* fallen—and had been caught by the authorities. All of my attempts to save her had accomplished nothing. I have no memory of my father in this experience but imagine he was just as mortified as I was.

Looking back, I must acknowledge that my mother was devoid of empathy for her children. It appears she never thought about how her criminal behavior might affect either Michele or me. I was particularly vulnerable at that time due to my age. By the time they enter kindergarten, just the age I was then, children are learning about autonomy from their parents, evaluating right from wrong, and developing responsibility for and a sense of pride in their actions. As an accomplice to my mother's crimes, what kind of pride could I feel in mine?

Yet moving from California to New Jersey was very exciting. It felt like a dream come true to live in Irvington, in my Grandma Gittel's home with my aunts, uncles, and cousins, sleeping on big mattresses in the middle of the floor and playing all the time. Or at least that was my initial reaction. At one time, there were eleven of us living in one rented bottom floor of a duplex. It must have been awful for the adults, but I was thrilled to be with my cousins!

I soon learned, however, that nothing good would come from living in such close quarters, as my parent's hostility toward each other grew more each day. I tried hard to hide their hostility from the rest of the family, primarily from my cousins. As I was a mere five years old, I have little understanding of how I thought I could accomplish that feat. I only know that I quickly learned to shoulder the blame for any transgressions our family made whenever I could. If anything went wrong, I apologized for it, making it my fault. It was always easy for me to assume the blame. Right or wrong, I always felt right being the one who was wrong. In fact, taking the blame for others' actions became such a deeply ingrained behavior that, as an adult, I have had to work very hard to *not* apologize. I must actually stifle the urge to do so, knowing that I am not responsible for everything. Today I know the true cause of my parents' conflicts throughout the years we lived in Irvington. My mother was so miserable in California that she had threatened to take Michele and I and move to New Jersey. My father knew there was no choice for him. I suppose in his eyes, we were still a family, but to accompany us did not lessen his anger at feeling pushed to make the move.

Soon, my cousins Maureen, Janice, and Lisa moved to their own home in Livingston, and within a short time, we moved into the two-bedroom apartment in Stuyvesant Village. I was six years old when we moved into our own apartment, and I was overjoyed. I remember jumping on the bed with excitement. It was January 1955, and my mother was extremely pregnant. Michele and I were very excited, particularly Michele because it was her turn to become a mommy.

Simply known as "the Village," these garden apartments had been rapidly built to accommodate the returning World War II veterans. We had waited for over a year for our two-bedroom apartment to finally become available. Unfortunately, moving to the Village was more responsibility than my father could handle. By now I was mature enough to notice that other dads went to work each day, but not mine. There were more and more days when I came home from school and he was still not awake. In his place, I found only a strange smell, the fetid odor of sleep. I remember asking my mother more than once, "Mommy, is Daddy sick?" "No," she replied, "he is very angry." Her explanation scared me so much, it made me never want to get angry. I vowed that I would never allow myself to become angry like my father, oh no.

Then when Michele was three and a half, she too was given her own baby doll, my sister Mindy Joy. Michele carried Mindy in her little arms the same way I had carried Michele, our sense of responsibility for one another far more acute than that of our parents. We continued to live in the Village until I was close to eleven, Michele eight, and Mindy five, and it was wonderful to share a room with both my sisters. The only problem was that it was difficult to keep our room as tidy as my mother wanted. I would watch her growing anxious and angry if any items were out of place. She would awaken us at all hours of the night—whenever she felt it necessary that we clean the room. So many Saturdays we would "surprise" her by cleaning without being told. That made all of us happy.

As soon as we grew old enough to manage, Michele (who was six or seven) would cook our breakfast and make our lunches. Meanwhile, at age nine or ten, I remained on hair detail. At one point, our family doctor mandated that my mother stay in bed in the mornings because she was unable to control her temper, and Michele, like me, had begun to suffer from stomach and intestinal issues, perhaps as a result of my mother's behavior. Mornings without my mother suited me very well. More than once the school nurse had called my father to pick me up when she couldn't stop the bleeding from my lip or cheek, split by my wild-eyed mother as she brandished her weapon—my hairbrush. Whereas my father's rage was planned and orderly, calmly asking for our hands or rear to smack, my mother's was frantic and furious. She smacked with whatever was in her hands or her fist. So frightened was I of upsetting either of them that I imagined it would cause the end of our family, the end of our lives.

In our new apartment, my parents still fought all the time. Their fights almost always began as conflicts about money, then escalated into physical screaming matches, their fingernails digging into and pinching each other until one parent finally left the room. Three children, rent, school clothes, and a poor wife who could never have anything of her own and wanted a new dress from time to time must have been more than my father could manage.

Even the arrival of the daily mail began to cause us all alarm, as my father's reaction to the stress of each envelope grew palpable. Then one day, the Bamberger's bill arrived and, with it, one of the most terrible fights I had witnessed in my young life. The amount of the bill was less the issue than the fact that my mother had used the emergency charge card to purchase herself a red dress for a party my parents were planning to attend. Once the screaming began, I shepherded my sisters into our bedroom to protect them, afraid that one of them would be caught amid the pushing in the middle of the living room. I stayed in the living room, as if to referee this bout.

My father demanded to see the red dress, which was stunning and would look wonderful on my mother. (I had seen it in the back of the closet when I went to take our clothes from the hamper earlier that day.) Pushing my father out of the way, my mother ran into their bedroom, and he followed with large steps to keep up with her. She pulled the dress from the closet, hoping, I suppose, that he would think it beautiful and leave her alone. My father took that dress, in his eyes the evidence of my mother's transgression, and he tore that gorgeous confection, with its high lace neck and lace sleeves, into pieces. She slapped and slapped him, and he slapped her back. Weeping and shaking, my sisters and I ran to our neighbor Mitzi's house and stayed there until my father came for us. It was hard to look at him but even harder not to do so. Years ago, when I reached out to Mitzi to ask about her memories of our family, she told me she had known my mother was terrified of my father and that she, Mitzi, had felt so sorry for my sisters and me. Hearing her perspective was both sad and validating. Still, I wanted to add that I believed my father had been equally as terrified of my mother. Their relationship was like a seesaw or a sliding board. One may be up and then down, down then up, but there was potential danger at all times.

My parents' pattern of fighting over money never ended, and we never became numb to it. One evening soon after the red-dress incident, my mother's brother, Uncle Jack, came for dinner. He was engaged and looking to begin a career. My father was to teach him the baby-picture business, since now, and I can only imagine how undependable his bosses found him, his profession was managing a few baby-picture salesmen. In those days, women didn't drive, so they couldn't go to photography studios, and most didn't have cameras available to take photos of their babies. So sending a professional photographer to women's homes every year for the first six years of each baby's life was a lucrative business model. It gave families access to special experiences and treasures they may not have otherwise had. The money was, of course, in the vast number of extra photos the families purchased for grandparents and the rest of the family. My Uncle Jack was anxious to work for my father, and I assume my father thought him capable of doing the job.

In our home, company was a rare occurrence, so we were excited Jack was now with us. As my mother prepared a tuna fish platter with cucumbers and carrots around the perimeter of the plate, we all prepared to sit at the crowded kitchen table. But my father took one look at the platter and asked why we weren't having steak, since we had a guest.

My mother told him it was too expensive and he hadn't left her enough money. "Because you bought yourself another dress?" he screamed. My sisters and I began to shake. My uncle stared straight ahead, obviously embarrassed. The fight soon escalated to the point of no control. All it took was one minute, and my father had thrown the beautiful platter of tuna fish, cucumbers, and carrots against the wall. In shock, we found ourselves unable to speak, and my uncle left.

For the first few decades of our marriage, Bruce and I rarely, if ever, fought. Looking back, it feels difficult to believe. Today I know it was because I had grown so numb to my parents' fighting that I felt arguing would never lead anywhere, and I had become a master at never getting angry. I suppose so had Bruce, for his own reasons. No doubt, I did not want my daughters to see or experience the violence I had seen and experienced growing up.

It took me years of therapy and awareness of the human experience to realize that getting angry and sharing that feeling with someone I love can bring us closer together and even make me more open to others' feelings. We can love others deeply, regardless of how differently they see the world. Over time, I also realized I had been painting an unrealistic picture for my girls, a picture that could lead them to believe that anger precludes a joyful and successful marriage. That insight took the longest for me to internalize, yet with trial and error, I eventually learned how to voice my anger in a controlled and caring way so that I didn't hurt or punish Bruce and he didn't retaliate by doing the same to me. It felt truly liberating to allow myself to embrace an emotion I had buried for decades. I had always been so fearful that expressing my anger would alienate me from people I love. Today I know that fear is no longer my reality. I can be my authentic self. In fact, those who love me actually desire that of me, and I no longer have to mask my true emotions in order to connect with others. As one of my therapists pointed out, when I am my true self, others want to know me better. A mask of perfection scares others away rather than brings them closer to me.

CHAPTER EIGHT
SCREECHING IN THE NIGHT

My sisters and I became attuned to the various sounds and appearances of my mother when she was in extremis. Her episodes arose from her disappointment, frustration, anxiety, and anger, from her feeling unloved, unheard, and uncared for. All our lives, we tried to tell her we loved her, but nothing we said was ever enough, and certainly, once she became ensconced in her unreality, became "that woman," there was nothing we could do to assuage her misery. Her histrionics proved commensurate with her distortion. Regardless of how we tried to show her love, she continued to feel unappreciated, unfulfilled, unsatisfied. Looking back, we rarely discussed the metamorphosis taking place, so conditioned were we to her unraveling—her casing, held tightly, now ripping at the seams.

As a child, I observed how she telegraphed her disappearance from reality. At times she would cover most of her lower face with lipstick. She ignored the outline of her lips, as if she couldn't fully see her own face, or as if she were looking at someone else, perhaps a clown, albeit a sad one, in the mirror. At other times she would release a screeching that resembled the powerfully high-pitched scream of an angry young child. That sound was frightening at any time of day—and horrifying in the middle of the night.

Sleeping soundly was elusive in our home. My sisters and I were always on guard. I referred to the hours between 2 a.m. and 4 a.m. as the bewitching hours, the time when my mother's familiar episodes frequently began. Pots and pans, if not washed sufficiently, crashed from the sink to the floor. The din of thrown-around plates or other errant, out-of-place items landing on the table or chairs often preceded her racing upstairs to our bedroom.

Her strong, adrenaline-driven arms heaved my sisters and me from the security of our beds. My mother was frenetic and driven, unable to hold back her anger. "Get up and clean that mess before I clean you for good!" she seethed. Regardless of our ages and how far we looked ahead, warding off events that might lead to danger was impossible. We never grew inured to the destruction our mother wrought upon us, nor were we ever successful in mitigating her anger, even as we became used to the pattens in her behavior and could predict their outcomes. My mother felt that any transgression was an act of war. Rather than discuss such a transgression at a time when we were all rational and my sisters and I were able to learn from whatever mistake we had made, my mother felt she had to address it at that moment. With her lack of self-control, she was akin to a toddler throwing a major tantrum. Sadly, at times she was equally unable to control herself with her friends. I remember her calling her closest friend at 2 a.m. to complain that she had paid ten cents more than she should have for lunch; my mother had ordered egg salad, which was less expensive than her friend's tuna.

And then, after brutalizing our night, belittling and attacking us, she would reach out to my sisters and I with her arms open, waiting to receive our loving hugs, kisses, and adoration, as if all the screaming that had just occurred had not just occurred. Then her crying would begin, her claims that we didn't love her, that we didn't care about her, that she was alone in this world. What followed was her sobbing that she had lost her father when she was only fourteen, that she had never had a mother who loved her, that we didn't love her either. There were times when one of us would hug her, one of us would run from the room, and one of us would start to laugh, so absurd and repetitive were her histrionics. Yet my sisters and I were always aligned in our feeling that there was no pleasing her. Regardless of how we reacted to her behavior, we could not make up for her childhood, for her losses in life. It was common knowledge she would have had us open our veins, all three of us, to have us transfuse our blood to her, if possible, so in need of us was she. Nothing was ever enough to give her, because she was never satisfied. She would tell us stories about mothers who had sacrificed themselves for their children and explain that those children had appreciated and loved their mothers—unlike us, who didn't show her enough love, enough appreciation.

Frequently, my mother would continue her rants until dawn, when reaching her fever pitch, her adrenaline propelling her to the telephone, she would call my grandmother Gittel to hurl familiar accusations.

"Mama, why don't you love me? Why don't you love my children?" my mother would screech. "You never loved my children. It's not Ellyn's and Michele's fault they were born in California." The heightened energy of her anger would awaken us from what little sleep we had gotten in between her middle-of-the-night outburst and this early-morning one, which always ended with my mother assuring us we were as unloved by her entire family as she was. Sadly, I felt numb then, hearing that I was unloved by my grandmother and by my extended family. The sound of pathos I heard in my ear was that of my mother's heart, not my own, breaking. My stomach did turn, however, as I thought of my tiny grandmother. As she spoke no English, she would whimper in Yiddish, "Lillian, I can't talk with you" and hang up the phone. As I listened, I felt that my grandmother had to be crying from the same frustration my sisters and I faced, all of us unable to satisfy the same unsatisfiable woman.

The end of my mother's morning fight with Gittel would prompt a phone call from whichever aunt or uncle was hosting my grandmother at that time: "Stop tormenting Mama, Lillian!" Then my mother's escalating rage would transfer from how my grandmother had never loved her or us to how our aunts and uncles didn't love us either.

"Your only grandparent doesn't love you, and they don't care because they don't love you either."

At that point, with bile rising in my throat, I would rock and steady my mother, consoling her, telling her that my sisters and I didn't care if no one else loved us, as long as she did. My mother appeared so helpless and needy that I was afraid to go to school and leave her in this vulnerable condition. I often say there is more love in a broken heart, and this poor, pitiful woman broke mine over and over again.

Since my sisters' and my school schedules varied over the years, there were times when one of us was still at home when my father finally awakened to my mother's screeching. Far from providing a comforting cushion for my mother's agony, he would instead pour acid into her emotional wounds.

"If you weren't so (fill in the blank: stupid, dumb, crazy), your mother would love you," he shouted at her. "Why should she love you? Why would anyone love you? I don't love you. Your daughters don't love you!" His attacks were so hateful that, even as a child, I saw how he loved having power over her, tormenting her.

I remember that my mother wanted to keep a kosher home, but my father would have none of it. Thus, my mother created her own method of observing her religious tradition. Besides eating kosher meat and chicken, she tried to safeguard her kosher status. She would cover her kosher meal with a piece of wax paper before setting her dish on her placemat on the table. But in order to "dirty" my mother's meal, my father would stab that wax paper and the food beneath with the tines of his fork, one he had used to eat nonkosher food. His violation of her religious practice was incredibly disrespectful, and it made me so angry. But there was no talking with him. Begging did no good. It only made him more determined to show his dominance, to prove to us he could get everything he wanted. I suppose he also wanted to show himself that he could dominate his wife, just as he dominated me with his lemons. I suppose it was also very important to him to show us we needed to stay on the right side of his aggression.

Heartbroken was the overriding emotion I felt throughout those years, all of my childhood and young adulthood, and still do as I reflect back on those decades until my father died when I was twenty. Despite her need to torment us, I didn't want my mother to be tormented. I wanted her to be loving, not lonely and beaten down by my father. So painful was that craving for a mother and father who would care for me that I became a wizard at pushing my anger at my parents down past my stomach and into my intestines. I lived on ever-stronger laxatives, but nothing gave me the ability to expel the demons that took ownership of my bowels. My parents were plagued with their own demons of rage, so how could I trust my mother or father to listen to mine? And how could I not feel guilt for selfishly wanting something from them they couldn't give themselves or each other?

My mother's constant heartbreak took center stage through most of our childhood, and I reflected on my overwhelming awareness of her needs for years afterward. When I was a young girl, my sadness and the chaos in which our family lived meant I had no concern for my appearance. When would I have had enough space to hold my appearance in my thoughts? Perhaps I wanted people to notice what a ragamuffin I felt I was. Perhaps I hoped to be rescued like a princess in a castle tower, transformed by anyone who cared. But I had no pride—where would I have learned that? All my parents ever showed me was what little value I had. All I ever felt was a disappointment to them. So I wore that moniker proudly, shouting my pain and grief. I wanted to be like the other girls, but I knew I was miles away from them. I wanted simply to hide.

By high school, however, I had become a master of deception. I suppose that metamorphosis reflected the physical changes in me and the positive attention I received from others when I reached out as my confidence grew. I built friendships with girls, and boys called for dates. Now that school was a true escape, I began looking at it as if I were a performer in a play.

Every school day felt like a piece of performance art in which I explored the question: *What could today be?*

Each morning, while I walked the school halls with my girlfriends, I would smile and say good morning to everyone I saw. I babysat constantly and bought a few nice things with my earnings. As was the fashion of the day, I wore madras shirts under fisherman sweaters with Bass Weejuns loafers and Adler socks. I embraced my femininity with Jean Naté or Ambush fragrance, Max Factor Pan Stik, and whatever soft-pink lipstick painted the picture of a young girl who had nothing on her mind but what was beautiful. I read all of the teen magazines so I was a master student of what would paint the picture of the "perfect teenager" who was well-adjusted, desirable, and blithely going through life.

Fooling my teachers proved more difficult. I put forth tremendous effort, but there were times when I felt vacant, absent of all motivation and concentration. While my grades were fine, I felt inferior to the higher-achieving girls in my classes. I pushed through challenges because I believed getting good grades was the best way to make my parents happy. Of course, their pleasure was always short-lived. My parents expected my sisters and me to perform well in school, but our achievements didn't really matter to their happiness, since whatever happened today could be eclipsed by something negative tomorrow. There was already another battle on their horizon.

Like me, my mother knew how to perform normalcy, acting according to the world's expectations for women. She was a genius in her ability to appear warm and friendly. Her smile was beautiful and inviting. Until it wasn't.

"Do not cross her" and "Do not let her down" were rules everyone had to follow around my mother. Any transgression could have devastating consequences. When Michele was about eleven, she had a friend, Barbara, who slept over at our house a few times. Our fathers were card-playing friends who had known each other for years, having grown up together. One night, wakening at around 3:30 a.m., my mother decided that Barbara had slept at our home one time too many, and she felt taken advantage of; Barbara had not reciprocated by inviting Michele to sleep at her home an equal amount, and it was time for her to leave. My mother awakened Barbara, threw her into the back of the car, drove her home, opened the door to the car, told her to "Get out!" and pulled away. My sisters and I all cried together, understanding the humiliation Michele must have been feeling. Gone was Michele's friend. Gone was any respect for our family.

CHAPTER NINE
THE OTHER WOMAN: ANITA

When I was nine years old, my father broke my heart.

Until then, it had never occurred to me that another woman could steal my father's love, a love my family had fought for and won so little of, but somehow Anita did.

Anita was a mystery. I did not know where she lived, what she looked like, what she watched on television or bought at the supermarket.

But I first suspected something was different by the way my father smelled. Forever, he had worn Aqua Velva, splashing it on his face after he shaved. Suddenly, he smelled not fresh and minty but like trees, or something from outside. While I couldn't identify his new scent, I knew he had changed, and I felt worried. So, although I didn't understand their cause, I was aware of the differences in him long before my mother accused him of infidelity. He began to look nice all the time, getting haircuts and wearing his shirt tucked into his belt, and yes, he smelled much different too.

That summer, my mother, sisters, and I were staying in a boarding house at Bradley Beach at the Jersey Shore. As was our custom, my father would "work" during the week and visit us each weekend.

We were so excited whenever Friday came; finally, our family would be complete. Yes, my father's visits always brought some tension, but I felt safer when he was with us than when he wasn't there. This particular weekend would be my sister Michele's sixth birthday, and we were all going to celebrate at Storyland Village, an hour from our boarding house. That Sunday morning, Michele wore a pink dress with flowers, and I styled her hair in braids, adding multicolored ribbons. I wanted her to feel like a princess. Mindy, three years old, was taking a nap so she would be at her best. (We were always one another's little mothers.) And my mother looked so pretty, as usual. She wore a plaid sundress, her small waist nipped in by a wide tan belt. Her lips were radiant in Revlon's Love That Red, her new favorite, and she had swept her golden-blonde hair into a French twist.

I had sensed something strange the past few weekends, and this one had me on alert the past few days. I couldn't put it into words, but by Sunday the feeling that something was wrong was building. My belly ached when I tried to figure out why. I knew my mother had become angrier and angrier at my father as the days had passed. Now Sunday morning, my ears pricked to the sounds of my parents behind their bedroom door. Sensing danger, I opened the door just enough to hear and see what was happening in their room. I wondered how I could salvage the situation, what responsibility I could take. There had to be something I could do to save Michele from sadness on her special day. Michele was the most generous person in my life. She gave me all her love, the only one who never disappointed me. Sometimes, my father would give us each a quarter to go down to the boardwalk and play in the arena. I was less careful with my quarter than Michele and dropped it through the slats of the boards a few times. "Here, Sistaw," she would say. "You can have mine." How could I allow her birthday to be ruined?

As my parents began screaming at each other about a woman named Anita, I began to shake. At nine years old, I was mature enough to suspect that whoever Anita was, she had to be a bad lady.

My mother hit my father in the chest, and he grabbed her wrists. I ran into the room screaming "Stop!" but my mother wouldn't. She continued to bang on his chest until she hurt him; the guttural sounds erupting from his lungs told me he was in pain. I wedged myself between my parents and jumped up, trying to protect my father, trying to let him know I loved him, the only way I could.

By now Michele was crying as she watched from the hall, and I heard Mindy awaken in our bedroom. My parents continued to fight, my mother pummeling my father as he pushed her away hard. Their fight seemed to last for hours, but it is likely they exhausted themselves long before that. Knowing I could do nothing more to stop the fight, I gathered my sisters and closed the door to our bedroom, and we cried, huddled together. Here we were, in a place far from our real home, with our parents attacking each other.

Eventually, my father opened the door and walked into the room, his head down, shoulders hunched. He told Michele that he would take her and me to Storyland Village, without my mother and Mindy. The three of us would have birthday cake there and go on rides. It would be "just us" celebrating her birthday. Always trying to do what I thought a mother would do, I took Michele's hand and grabbed sweaters for both of us. My mother didn't come out of her room, so we brought Mindy to her. Tears were running down her face, and she had a peculiar look about her. I was afraid to leave Mindy, but my father said it would be okay.

It was the saddest day I could remember. My father cried while he drove to Storyland Village, he cried while we were on the rides, he cried while we ate our birthday cake with white frosting and pink and purple sprinkles. He cried on the way home, he cried when he walked in the door, and he cried while he tried to sleep on the couch. I came out in the middle of the night and put a blanket on him.

We had looked forward to Michele's birthday all summer, but I never got the sense that he cried because he was sorry for ruining her special day. He cried out of regret, I assume, for his own behavior. Or perhaps he cried with frustration that he and my mother fought every weekend when he finally arrived. Or perhaps he cried for a million other reasons I was too young to understand or intuit.

However he felt that day, it was a turning point for me. As hard as it might be to imagine, I understood by the end of the weekend, at only nine years old, that my father had fallen from grace by choosing another woman. We had always received so little of his love, and now he had given away even more to a stranger. If he could choose her over us, then what else could he do to break our hearts? I resolved to hold on to my heart much tighter than ever before. Perhaps in my own way, I felt as crushed as my mother. And then my guilt set in, my guilt at feeling angry and at not wanting to love him. These feelings have never left me. Turning a corner, I could not go back to the person I had been.

Michele's birthday celebration was in the beginning of August, and we returned home soon after. Although my father promised to end it with Anita, she continued to appear in my nightmares, and perhaps in my mother's as well.

My mother may have acted resigned and accepting, forgiving and forgetting, but that was not her reality. She was a woman with a desire for revenge, perhaps that was the look I saw on her face, and she would not let go of her husband's betrayal.

One Sunday morning in early September, I heard a loud knock on our apartment door. Eager to see who was knocking, I ran out of my bedroom—I loved when we had company. My mother went to the door and opened it. She seemed not at all surprised to see her brother and brother-in-law standing there. If I had been older, I might have recognized a conspiring glance, but I was too excited to see two of my uncles at our home at the same time—I had no memory of both of them ever visiting us together before.

My father walked out of the bedroom in his sleeveless undershirt and undershorts. Suddenly, my uncles grabbed him and began beating him with their fists. Finally, they left him bloody and in shock. This was retribution for his wandering. My mother's revenge. She watched in silence, a look of supremacy on her face. I was terrified into silence.

Throughout my childhood, I rarely felt like a child, but after that day, I never felt like a child again. I had grown up, seeing my greatest fears come to life. My father had been beaten. My mother had been betrayed, and then she betrayed him, using her family to badly harm my father. From then on, I lived in fear of physical violence.

My mother reached into the freezer and took out a frozen steak to apply to the black eye now angrily bulging above my father's left cheek. Her calm was unnerving. She had that otherworldly look on her face, the look that revealed she was in her own place now and none of us were part of it. Perhaps her gaze was rapturous. She must have felt the sweetness of her revenge on my father for his betrayal. But why would she violate the trust of her children? Why would she betray us? And why would she have this beating in front of us?

I never heard Anita's name again. But many years later, at my father's shiva, my uncles told me my father had sworn he never actually had an affair. He claimed to have created the entire fantasy because my mother was distant and difficult. He thought making her jealous would help improve their marriage. He was obviously as lost in wanting to be loved by her as we.

As an adult, I don't care if the Anita affair was fact or fantasy. The beating I witnessed was terrifying and appalling. Most devastating of all was the new awareness this act of violence sparked in me: My father was powerless to defend himself against my mother's abuse. If even our father had no way to combat my mother's icy rage besides betraying us, then what chance did we, his young daughters, have at feeling safe?

Today I recognize that my father must have felt so powerless, whether or not he created a scenario of infidelity, loving another woman more than his own family. I have no doubt that my father never felt himself on terra firma with my mother, so incapable of coping with her behavior were we all. Maybe he needed to feel like a "man." How sad that if he did create this affair, it had to impact us, his children, and how especially sad that his lies had to unravel on Michele's birthday. Yet interestingly, over time, my father's affair has become just one more horrific experience I remember. I am so grateful his betrayal of me as a child has not determined the course of my adult relationships.

I knew Bruce would never act as my father did. From the beginning, Bruce had too much self-respect and nothing to prove to me, or to himself. We talked many times over the years about "opportunities" each of us had and the commitment we had made to each other. That commitment included a choice to be faithful and stay together, and we agreed that straying would put all of the love we shared and the children we cherished at risk. We knew that a transgression would incur devastating consequences. I remember thinking many times that trust is the first accomplishment an infant achieves and must be a lifelong treasure. If we cannot trust each other to honor our commitment, how can we build a foundation for a lasting relationship?

Still, when Bruce and I had children, my memories of my parents' actions when I was nine years old remained within me. When Allison was nine years old, she had to have a laser procedure, so I took her to the hospital myself. I didn't ask or even consider having my partner, my husband, her father, join us. I was so certain I could care for her myself. Attempting to care for Allison in the hospital by myself proved a terrible choice. My poor daughter was in pain and traumatized. I soon grew so angry at myself for not providing her with more support than me alone that I went back into therapy to understand my guilt and my resistance to include Bruce in parenting. As "the mother," I had wanted to handle it all, to prove to my own mother that I didn't need to rely on anyone, including her! How brazen, and how foolish I felt when I recognized I had served no one by trusting only myself. All I had done was prove to myself what poor judgment I had.

There were so many times when I felt like a canoe adrift alone on the ocean, unsure of how to parent, yet afraid to "impose" upon Bruce, busy building his career, for assistance. This was the biggest mistake of all for me and my daughters, and I suppose for him as well. Part of me wonders if it was easier for me to go it alone, but the other part of me wonders if, perhaps, I felt if I asked for help, I would be denigrated like my mother. Replicating the interactions of my parents was a huge fear, but that fear prevented me from getting the support I needed and Allison and Emily from feeling the strength and guidance of their father. Looking back, each issue was my focus in therapy, and I was totally committed to changing my behavior with every fiber of my being as I processed and developed coping skills. Many changes and coping skills may have come too late in certain situations, and this, I strongly believe, is one of them.

CHAPTER TEN
SHOULDERING RESPONSIBILITY

As I locked the memories of my father's affair, or lack of it, deep in my heart, my feelings became even more strongly aligned with my mother's. Sadly, I felt I had to choose a side, and although my mother was irrational and volatile, my father had given his love, the love we desperately needed, to another woman. My mother must have asked my uncles to avenge her honor, of that I have little doubt, but as a preteen, it seemed more in keeping with being a good daughter to align myself with her. The relationship we developed was a perfect combination of her self-pity and my overwhelming need to protect her. I saw her as my charge to keep alive. I vowed to never allow her to succumb to the misery and distrust I suspected she must have felt after the affair—and which, in fact, I may have been avoiding feeling myself. Neither of my parents ever talked with me about the affair, nor did anyone else until my father's shiva, when my two uncles shared his plea that there had never been an Anita.

While my parents' fights remained a constant part of our family's daily life, my sisters and I grew to tune them out as often as possible. My mother pinched my father, as she pinched us. But he pinched back, something we could never do. He took to his bed with regularity, regardless of how many bills were being delivered in the mail. Life felt as if it were teetering on a tinder box. How would we survive? Additionally, as an adult, I cannot watch violence of any kind on television or in movies and have gotten physically sick when caught unaware of something I did not anticipate.

Even "scary music" makes me feel ill. Bruce has told me many times it surprises him that I am strong and brave when others would be unable to cope, and yet watching something on a screen, something not even real, makes me so weak, I often need to leave the room or theater.

And then, when I was ten, we moved into a new home on the other side of Union. No longer renting an apartment and "throwing away money," somehow we were able to afford to move to our home. A fresh start. And I would have my own bedroom, while my sisters would share theirs. I am certain the financial stress of buying a house must have felt enormous for my father, a man with little drive to earn a living. One of the gifts my father had, however, was his salesmanship, and even in his limited effort to work, he mastered enough sales to maintain some salary. Managing a few other salesmen, he eked out a living, enough that we had a new home.

My mother must have also felt tremendous stress. She would need to manage a home that was larger and more expensive than the apartment, furnish the house, interact with our neighbors, and establish a new life. I had my own adjustments to make: a new school, new friends, and new rules for how to navigate this new community. My sisters were navigating their own changes. Still, each of my parents reacted to our family's move from their own perspective, unconcerned with the adjustment of the other members of the family. As always, my parents' lives were primarily driven by their needs, their goals, their desires. My sisters and I were always collateral damage.

In our new home, my parents had a terrible fight, which ended as usual, with my father retreating to his corner of the boxing ring, his bed. When he was gone, my mother clawed at my sisters and me, her feelings of rejection particularly difficult to ignore. I could feel my mother begging us to love her, to shower her with emotions, to cry for her sadness. But my sisters and I were caught up in our own desires to fit into our new neighborhood. My mother tried everything, reminding us that her father had died when she was fourteen years old, that she had been forced to leave school and go to work, that my father degraded her lack of education, and on and on. Her pleas felt overwhelming, but so many days were.

Yet this fight proved particularly decisive. Afterward, my parents did not speak to each other for weeks. The pall that fell over our home felt oppressively frightening. The contrast between the excitement my sisters and I had felt moving into a new home and the hostility my parents now exhibited in our house resembled a grosgrain ribbon, its striations beautiful on top while coming unwoven beneath.

Walking to school one crisp November morning, only a few weeks into the new school year, I shuffled my feet to slow down my progress. I was guiding Michele to our elementary school, and she didn't walk as quickly. Dropping her off at her designated door, I heaved a sigh of relief, knowing she had been safely delivered. Her safety was, of course, my responsibility.

Then I walked to the door where the older students waited. We were sixth graders, a big deal since this was our last year before junior high school. The boys were, as usual, monopolizing the playground and adjacent spaces while flirting with the popular girls. I had yet to integrate into the social fabric of the class. In this slightly more affluent area, I felt different from the other girls around me. I didn't have the same clothes as the girls in my class: full skirts, Peter Pan collared blouses, black cinch belts, ballerina slippers. The girls in charge of the social scene all looked as if they stepped out of the very same closet. I was wearing a red corduroy jumper with big white buttons at the straps and an itchy faded-black turtleneck sweater. I was the epitome of unsophisticated among a sea of girls who seemed to have it all. I had grown up in an apartment, and these girls lived in homes. Having gone to school together for years, these girls had formed a clique, and they readily dismissed new people. I had little self-esteem, and it showed in my posture and my appearance. I felt less than everyone.

Deepening my isolation, my mother's voice shrieked in my head. I constantly worried about how sad she was. And I was worried about our family's bills. Who would pay them now that my father was even more often asleep? Among my more comfortable classmates, I felt like a fish out of water. I wished I could disappear as I huddled to get warm in the doorway in between the big, heavy entrance door and the wall of the school. All at once, without warning, that industrial-sized door, meant to protect the kids inside from the dangers of the outside world, was pushed open, and I found myself trapped in the corner.

The biggest boy in the school was demonstrating his strength, and my small body proved no match for the power with which he had launched that door outward. I remember hearing what sounded like the button on my jumper cracking. However, it was not my button but my right clavicle, or collarbone, breaking as my shoulder was dislocated. Suddenly, my arm was hanging out of my turtleneck sweater, my books thrown askew onto the cold pavement.

Falling to the ground heaving and vomiting, I went into shock. I can still picture the sun peeking between the clouds as I heard voices telling me to focus, but my gaze remained unsteady. The clouds were dancing, and my head was spinning, and then, like a bolt of lightning from those clouds, the pain became excruciating. I began to whimper, then sob, then scream in horror. I did not recognize the feral sounds I was making, didn't even realize they were emanating from my throat.

The school nurse's office became a hub of activity, but I sat stoically rooted to my chair with a bag to catch any remnants of my nausea. When the nurse called my parents, at first my mother informed her that she didn't drive and my father was not home. I remember my pain felt extraordinary, and it increased in waves of agony every time I moved. More time must have passed than I realized because suddenly, I saw my parents at the door of the nurse's office. Then my tears turned to racking sobs.

My father had been home, of course, still sleeping off the fight he and my mother had been having for the past few weeks. I knew my mother must have dragged him out of bed, perhaps pulling him by his hair. As troubled as they were, their child was hurt, and that pain had brought my parents together—*I* had brought them together. I must admit, I felt a bit heroic, having aroused my father from his reverie and brought my parents here to take care of me. Watching them walk into the nurse's office, not holding hands but still united in their concern for me, I was filled with relief, despite my horrific pain.

One Thanksgiving, a few years before my accident, my father was playing touch football with my uncles, the same ones who had beaten him up not long before, when he fell on the pavement, landing hard on his shoulder and collarbone. His fractures were horrible, and his agony palpable. My sisters, my mother, and I all cried as my uncles carried him to the car and took him to the hospital. We waited up for him late that night, terrified he would not return. Afterward, we cared for him as if he were made of the most fragile china, his wife and three young daughters all nursing him through his pain.

Coincidentally, my parents brought me to the same hospital emergency room that my father had been in years before. I tried to be as brave as I imagined my father to have been. But my pain, like his, was unrelenting. By the time we were able to see the doctor, I was exhausted. The doctor offered us a choice: either a brace and a sling or a surgery that would allow the orthopedist to pin my completely cracked collarbone and set my dislocated shoulder back in place. Fearing that an unsightly scar and a visible pin would cause me emotional pain when I matured and wanted to wear more revealing clothing, my parents chose the less aggressive approach—no surgery. Unfortunately, after wearing that brace for close to two and a half years while my body developed into young womanhood, I believe surgery would have offered me a more rapid and complete recovery. Even in my late twenties, I dealt with the effects of the dislocation. Eventually, the body heals, scar tissue created, but I dealt with muscle spasms for years into adulthood.

As awful as the entire experience was, its silver lining was quite bright and beautiful. My parents became unified in their desire to help me. They listened to the directions given by the doctor, brought me to appointments, wrapped me, and helped me wash and get ready for school in the mornings. They worked as a team—until that responsibility too, of course, became too much for them. But my father knew the pain I suffered, having suffered it himself, and so he and my mother maintained a détente for a period of time. I needed a lot of physical attention to bathe and get dressed for school, so my parents worked out a daily schedule, a regular morning routine in which my father was, by necessity, heavily involved. I was responsible for the peace of those few weeks, until my parents no longer could sustain it. I was responsible for my parents coming together to help each other help one of us. I became the recipient of milkshakes and comic books and grew seduced by the attention I received. And I admit I was grateful. I was grateful for all of the pain I endured and, particularly, for the knowledge that it had brought my family together; although my right shoulder was terribly injured, shouldering that responsibility had given me a purpose that filled me with gratitude!

That experience was on my mind when my daughter Allison was hospitalized at ten months old, having spiked a fever of over 106 degrees. I had run high temperatures myself as a child and feared that Allison's fever might rise even higher. So when her pediatrician suggested Allison's condition be monitored, I immediately rushed my daughter to the hospital. I rocked her hot little body, told her how much I loved her, and nuzzled her neck. When the nurse told me to undress her and leave her uncovered, then rubbed her with cool compresses, her body shivering, I cried as Allison cried. I remembered my parents crying when I was in the hospital with that awful shoulder pain. I still remember thanking them over and over again for taking care of me, something regardless of my child's age, I would never expect her to do.

My doctor and I knew each other quite well when I had my shoulder accident, and I continued to see him a few times a week for heat treatments to enhance the healing of the bone. I have no idea if that helped in any way, but he was a comfortable person in my life. He seemed to sense that for all the years he knew me, my body was struggling. My shoulder was a challenge, but we all believed it would eventually heal. What felt less certain was how to treat the boulder I felt lying in the pit of my stomach and how it impacted my bowels. What I have learned over the years is that the gastrointestinal system has its own central nervous mechanism and reacts to stimuli over which we may have little control.

My poorly functioning intestines, sadly, always brought me to Dr. Shapiro's office and, sadly, always yielded the same results. "Nerves." Eventually, he ordered tests to better validate his belief that I did not have a disease he should treat.

Today, there are a myriad of tests and abilities to diagnose intestinal issues, and I say this as one who has had most of them. However, in the 1950s, the gold standard was to either drink barium, a chalklike substance, and I mean it actually tasted like chalk as well as looked like it, and x-ray it as it flowed down or pump it into the rectum and to the colon, taking X-rays as it flowed up. Barium was a great tool, despite its awful taste, but when it lay in the body, it became concrete. For a person with immotile bowels, it was nearly impossible to pass it for days, cramping terribly as the body tried to rid itself of the foreign substance. Fortunately, today's preparations are very different. The use of CT scans, MRIs, ultrasounds, and other means of obtaining diagnostic information all utilize better-metabolized methods of illumination.

I sat on the cold dark metal slab of a table, readying myself for my first barium enema. I was close to eleven years old, and the adult-sized hospital gown hung below my feet. I had tripped over the excess material as I walked to the cold X-ray table.

Irvington General Hospital sat on a hill overlooking Chancellor Avenue, a long and winding road traversing Essex County. It was the same avenue where my mother had shoplifted years before, and where we had been caught by the police. The radiology department was in the basement of the hospital building. I looked through the bottom of a high window that allowed me to see the feet of people walking by, and I wished I could be outside with them. Alone, I waited for the procedure designed to validate that my colon had anomalies, which, of course, it did.

The poor radiology technician, a young man tasked with inserting the nozzle end of the enema tube filled with barium into my small rectum, must have also had nightmares after that day. The chalky white substance, in a huge tub, apparently required one more stir before he was able to siphon it into the bag, and the technician made struggling sounds as he worked to accomplish the task. I knew the thick liquid had to be heavy. I resigned myself to whatever was coming. Pulsating rivers of barium entered, stopped, then entered again. *Deep breath, hold your breath.* More barium entered. *Stop.* He gave me instructions for what felt an eternity, and I pretended I was escaping a fight between my parents, leading my sisters out of the house, needing to be very strong. *Deep breath, hold your breath, breathe.*

My abdomen blew up like a balloon. When the hellish procedure was over, I rocked on the table, agony washing over me. Concrete ... getting my flaccid, angry bowels to push it out became an impossibility that night or the next, or the next. Having anticipated a soap enema, I nearly burst out crying. But I was determined to be a good girl.

Dr. Shapiro called and told us to come see him when I felt better. The barium enema showed that I had a megacolon, meaning enlarged, with a redundant foot off the transverse colon. A rambling, spastic, tortured structure was the anatomical description. I was tortured, so although I was only close to eleven years old, it was no surprise my anatomy reflected it.

And so my childhood was a nightmare of attempts to force my bowels to move. Soap enemas, colonic mixtures, and other laxatives took part in my everyday life. I became accustomed to years of soap enemas (a bar of soap melted in hot water filling a rubber enema bag with a long tube and a nozzle not designed for a child), and when these no longer did the job, my mother took my sisters and me on bus trips to a pharmacy several towns away from our home to drink a colonic mixture only a pharmacist could create. My mother would walk the three of us the two miles to the bus, heaving my sister Mindy's stroller up onto the top of the bus platform. It is impossible for me to describe the anxiety I felt as

I anticipated the impending drink of castor oil mixed with who knows what terribly strong laxative, so terribly difficult to swallow. Then the bus ride back, followed by the two mile walk home. My father never offered to drive us to the pharmacy—he was sleeping. And like many women at that time, my mother didn't drive—driving was considered a privilege for men and an expense that many homes could not afford. Unfortunately, returning to our apartment, with its one bathroom, only added to the misery I associated with my intestines for years.

My anatomy was clearly against me, but the stress my unstable parents produced in me exacerbated my slow motility throughout my life—of that I have no doubt. Every problem in our family became my constant worry. From the time I was a toddler, I was a guard, standing straight and tall, attempting to become my family's consummate protector. Incessantly, I worried that my father would leave or my mother would die, leaving my sisters and me with nobody to care for us. I worried that I wouldn't be enough when my sisters needed me. I worried that we would have no money and have to leave our home. And worst of all, I worried that my parents would hurt themselves or each other, or even one of us. Apparently, my bowels paid the price.

Managing this combination of anatomical and emotional stress was challenging. My intestines reacted constantly—to anxiety, food, sleep, medication, travel, and a myriad of other influences. Revealing my stress to others often caused more concern, as I was constantly reminded that my tortured colon represented my tortured soul. I did not want to be someone who made others uncomfortable or be seen as struggling. That desire to be a "whole person," which was something I rarely felt, took a tremendous amount of psychic energy and, perhaps, physical as well.

As I matured, I visited several physicians who told me to eat three balanced meals a day, never vary my diet, add fiber, and drink lots of fluids, but none ever addressed the impact of emotional stress. None ever even asked if I was facing stress at home. Did I need to talk with a professional about any issues? I still believe that, regardless of what I did at mealtimes, the way my body reacted to stress remained the key variable influencing my physical health and the one variable that, sadly, I could not control.

Years later, in 2001, as I prepared to have my colon removed at the Mayo Clinic in Rochester, Minnesota, I had a series of three warm-water soap enemas before I donned my surgical gown. In the preparation room, there were others having the same cleanse who complained about the torturous and mystifying practice. Yet I found myself returning to the times in my life when my mother did what she could to help me, to provide what I needed, to support me, to love me. I remembered her holding my shoulder in place in the emergency room when I broke my collarbone. I remembered her putting forth a herculean effort, transporting three of us, a stroller included, to take me to the pharmacy to obtain the colonic mixtures in order to ease my pain. I remembered her performing the soap enemas, which I assume were quite an effort for her. As I leaped upon the gurney that would take me to the operating room, the nursing staff teased me that I was the most joyful patient they ever had. I have always been joyful when I feel loved.

Today, I am joyful when I share my knowledge, understanding, and empathy with the members of my ostomy support groups and with the individuals I mentor, and especially when I can help new ostomates who feel frightened, certain they will never master their new anatomy or feel happiness again. I meet each patient where they are and assure them they will look back with pride in their accomplishments. They will adjust and possibly even mentor others. I am told my positivity has been a catalyst for the success that many people in my community feel today. I deeply appreciate their gratitude. But the gratitude I feel as a patient works through the challenges of their adjustment is equally exhilarating for me!

CHAPTER ELEVEN
DINNER WITH DONNA'S FAMILY

I remember the first moment I allowed myself to wonder, to ponder straying from the protection of our "secret party line." Did I have the right to wonder? The question of how my parents were different from those of my friends had always been there, waiting in the back of my mind. On that night, the darkness enveloped me, and I felt the chill in the November air. Decades later, I remember little about how Donna and I got the lava to spew from our handmade volcano, but I will always remember the feelings that erupted in me.

I was almost twelve years old, and Donna and I were both in the seventh grade. We were working on a science project together. Since I felt too worried to invite her into my home to finish our project, I was relieved when Donna invited me to hers. It was always my responsibility to consider, with careful concern, my father's sleeping status. I knew he would be furious if he awakened to find a stranger in the house. I could not predict what might happen if one of my friends happened to observe his car in the driveway, his pants hanging from the closet door, the acrid smell of sleep permeating the house, the tension in my mother. My parents only rarely gave my sisters and me permission to have friends over, and we almost never invited visitors into our home without my parents' explicit permission.

Donna lived close to our junior high school if we walked the back woods to her house. We knew we should never walk alone along "the path," but walking with friends felt safe, as naive as that feeling actually was. The path ran through swampy land, a perfect place for people on the run. I had heard the stories told and retold, stories of criminals hiding in the swamp, and only those with bravado would walk that path alone. Years later, reading the book *The Lovely Bones* by Alice Sebold, I saw in my mind's eye *our path*, come alive, with all of its danger.

Entering Donna's home felt unusual. There were crucifixes in each room, unlike the mezuzah my family displayed on our outer door. However, I quickly noticed a warmth inside that felt seductive to me, and I felt my body relax. Donna's mother offered each of us a small biscuit and a glass of cold milk, and then, in her broken English, she told Donna to invite me to stay for dinner. Thrilled by this invitation, I immediately answered yes. In response, Donna's mother told Donna to have me call my mother, ask permission, and find out what time a parent would come pick me up, since it would be too dark for me to walk home after dinner.

Taking the phone from Donna's hand, I began to calculate: What were the chances my mother would care if I came home or not (she wouldn't), and what were the chances that either of my parents, since my mother now drove, would pick me up at Donna's house (they wouldn't)? But I wasn't going to let this opportunity to have a nice dinner with Donna and her family pass, so I said all of the appropriate things. I was good at pretending. I thanked her mom from mine, appreciating her hospitality, and stated out loud I would call for that ride I knew I would not receive. Even if my mother had said he would pick me up, my father would not do so. "Let her walk home if it is so important to eat at her friend's," he would likely argue.

Donna's father, a quiet man, returned from work just as we put the finishing touches on our project. He kissed his wife and his mother, who lived with them, then Donna and her brother. He handed his lunch box to his wife, which she opened and dropped into the sink filled with bubbly suds. He acknowledged me with a nod and washed up before we all sat down for dinner.

Meeting him was difficult for me. Although he seemed nice, I felt I knew better what fathers were really like, just as I knew that regardless of how much Donna's mother pretended to care about her family, her act could only last so long. My goal was to eat and leave before everyone became the people whom I expected them to become. However, the softness of Donna's mother and father, their quiet way of being, and their gentle interest in me and my family—their questions about how many sisters I had and what Donna and I were doing with our project—felt so comforting that I hated to think of leaving.

Donna's house smelled of warmth, happiness, and spices, and we had the most delicious dinner. Oregano, basil, pepper, Italian breadcrumbs, and grated cheese created the most wonderful scents to me, and my nose almost tickled from the combination. My family's meals, in addition to being punctuated with misery, never smelled like this one, inviting me to the table. I can still smell those hamburgers, mixed with the aromatic combination of herbs and other ingredients. I can still hear them bouncing around in the heat of the big black skillet until they arrived at our plate, incredible. I sensed that Donna's mom had actually included another ingredient, one I had rarely tasted, and that was love. My hamburger roll, another treat that was forbidden in our home ("A moment to the lips, a lifetime to the hips!") felt soft and moist, and the cold glass of milk that accompanied the family's conversation at the table felt captivating. I listened intently as Donna's parents asked what Donna and her brother had learned in school that day, and I was so pleased that Donna's grandmother smiled when I glanced over at her. Looking back, I realize that the feeling I had listening to the banter, quiet and simple as it was, filled me with a warmheartedness I still remember, decades later.

After dinner I called home. I was hoping for a change of heart, but I received the response I had expected, the same one I was used to receiving from my parents: "Walk home." Accustomed to pretending, I waited the fifteen minutes it would have taken my parent to drive to Donna's home, if one had chosen to do so. Then, having thanked Donna's family profusely, I left with my books and my part of the project.

Standing on Donna's porch, I pressed my ear so close to the doorjamb that my skin quickly grew chilled. I felt my thoughts becoming obsessive. If I waited just a little longer, then I would hear the yelling inside begin, proving my suspicion that Donna's family was like mine after all. Yet for as long as I stayed in that position, I never heard any noise. Surely, if her father were screaming at her mother, or vice versa, I would have heard it. I had intruded into their home; how could they tolerate that intrusion? What if her father had been sleeping when I arrived? Or what if her mother had cut the tomatoes too thick, the ketchup bottle had been too dirty, or she had used the wrong knife and it had ruined his appetite? Donna's mother would be punished, as would Donna and her brother. Then her mother, in retaliation, would start slapping Donna, pinching, screeching, and yelling, punishing effects of her transgressing by bringing me home. How much longer? How could they pretend so well? I finally left.

Years later, Michele told me she had done exactly the same thing at her best friend's home. "I pressed my ear to the doorframe for so long, it left an imprint on my skin. I, too, was compelled to hear the screaming!" she explained.

Walking home in the dark was a frightening danger with which I was to become all too familiar, as my parents continued to use rides to and from friends' houses as weapons or rewards. But that night in November, as cold and scared as an eleven-year-old could be, having eaten the most delicious hamburgers and met a family skilled at perhaps pretending to care about one another and about me, I felt exquisite joy. Heavy with the weight of my books and the oaktag volcano, laden with paper-mache, I had a long time to consider the evening as I walked the two miles home. Donna had no idea, I was certain, of the freedom she had to bring a friend home to work on a project. She could not have known how different our homes were—at my house, the same action would have likely evoked my parents' wrath. Donna could not have known how much it meant to me when her mother invited me to stay for dinner as we sat calmly around the table, and when her father was, it seemed, so welcoming, interested in Donna and me and in what we had accomplished. How I had sat with my back straight against the dining room chair and used all my best manners, my heart filled with gratitude. I still remember every one of my senses coming alive that day.

The warmth of Donna's family changed me deeply. I realized that my senses had become muted at home. I had told myself that all families were like mine, but clearly, they were not. Our meals were painful at times, and stressful all the time. As an adult, I have so often grieved what could have been for the three of us, my sisters and I, had we grown up feeling secure rather than feeling we needed to protect ourselves from our parents. I suppose the layer of numbness I developed at a young age protected me even as it robbed me of happiness and enjoyment throughout my childhood.

Today, dinners with friends and family are my treasures. The ability to enjoy a meal, talk about our lives, share our emotions, or simply get to know new people as one opens a new book, learning all of their chapters, is such a gift, one that I greatly appreciate.

My awareness of the contrast between Donna's home and mine has stayed with me all these years. These days, I admit, I think less about the delicious smells of the hamburgers, pungent with oregano and basil, which I have never found replicated anywhere, than about the difference in the behaviors of our families. Had my parents not been so limited in their abilities to parent, I could have invited Donna to my house to do our science project, my mother would have made a delicious dinner, and there would have been no anger, fights, or emotional outbursts. My sisters and I would have had the luxury of growing up in a home that was not always dark with shame, shrouded in humiliation.

That dinner with Donna's family was a fateful night for me. That was the night I could pretend no longer. That was the night I learned to hide my shame, and I would continue to hide it for decades. That night, more than any other, was the night that forced me to grow up.

CHAPTER TWELVE
WAKE UP, DADDY

I can't remember why he took to his bed this time, only that the house had an awful pall over it. The stench of sleep, darkness, and pain—all familiar—for some reason felt particularly distressing on this day. I was seventeen, and I wanted to bring a friend home to study for a test, but as I have explained, nobody was allowed in the house while my father was visibly depressed. The shame we felt when my father retreated from our family made all of us feel that we needed to hide. None of us wanted to threaten the veil that protected us from the eyes of others.

After nine days without my father, we tried to awaken him, my mother slamming doors and the rest of us gathering outside his room, even loudly discussing his favorite foods: pizza, steamed clams, black raspberry and coffee ice cream. Nothing aroused him from his miasma. Nothing brought him back to us.

And then, something did.

As we prepared for dinner that night, we heard him in the shower. Perhaps it was the smell of sizzling meat wafting to his sleeping nostrils that had awakened him, or perhaps it was simply his untenable hunger. Either way, he came down to the kitchen smelling not of sleep, but of green Palmolive soap and Aqua Velva—glorious!

Abuzz with excitement, we quickly added his plate, glass, fork, and steak knife to our table. We had so much to share with him, having missed him throughout those nine days. Perhaps that was our mistake, our giddy enthusiasm, too much for a man with limited coping skills returning from his Rip Van Winkle escape. I do not know what was happening in his mind, only that he became more and more distant. While he entered the kitchen looking handsome and radiant, the more eager we grew to receive from him any attention he might offer, the more his mood deteriorated. He sat at the table in a trance. Trying to engage him in conversation only caused his eyes to flutter, as if he were trying to focus on us but couldn't.

Soon he stared straight ahead, unresponsive. He was sitting across from Mindy, usually the best of all of us at drawing him out of his isolation, so at first I assumed his eyes were focused on her. But this turned out to be only a wish. He was somewhere else, somewhere very dark, in a mood I was entirely unable to identify. The usual light in his eyes had vanished as if it had never existed; in fact, he made no eye contact with any of us at all. Holding his fork and knife, he awaited the steak my mother was broiling, the kitchen filling with smoke from the oven, the fans whirling. Still in a trance, he began to raise and lower his utensils. I felt as if I were watching a movie in slow motion.

Perhaps he was trying to remember what he was doing at the table. My mother had set out the ketchup and A.1. Steak Sauce bottles, messy as usual, with liquid dripping down the sides—they annoyed him, he pointed out in the few words he was able to speak. Then my mother brought the steaks to the table and placed one on his plate. He raised his sharp steak knife as if to make the first cut. Instead, he pushed his palm down onto the blade.

We screamed in unison, "Don't do that! Daddy, don't! You're hurting yourself!"

Instead of stopping, he seemed more determined to continue. His hand was dripping blood when he finally lifted it off the point of the knife. He reminded me of Rod Steiger in *The Pawnbroker*, the character who wanted to actually feel something. Perhaps that was the crux of his violence against himself—he was as numb as I felt at times.

But now my mother, my sisters, and I were all crying hysterically. Apparently unable to tolerate our sobbing, my father took his knife, slowly climbed the stairs to our bathroom, turned on the water, and locked the door. He did not respond to my sisters and me begging him through the door to let us help him. My mother remained in the kitchen. My sisters and I sat at the door for the longest time, crying, pleading, then finally accepting that he was determined to end his life—that was why he had awakened. To this day, I have no memory of why we simply curled up outside the door to the bathroom, sitting watch, tangled together like newborn puppies, and didn't call the police for help. Maybe it was because we were so used to dealing with everything ourselves, maybe we were frightened they would take him away and he would never forgive us, or maybe we were certain this was what he wanted, to end it all!

Eventually, after what felt like hours but was probably no more than a half of one, the door opened. Ignoring our agony, my father walked past us, his three daughters. My mother was still down in the kitchen praying out the open window over the dinner dishes in the sink. She prayed in a gibberish we never understood. It was neither Hebrew nor Yiddish but a combination of words and sounds that never made sense; my sisters and I could only determine that she was introducing herself to G-d and promising him she would never do anything wrong again.

Then my father took off his pants, hung them on the door of their closet, his customary hanging spot, and got into bed without a word. No one ever discussed the "incident." As usual, life resumed.

I must tell you this story because it reveals the depth of my father's agony. This night was different from the times he angrily chased my mother around the house, accusing her of spending too much money, or raged at me because he believed I had actually stolen money from him, when in fact, I had lied to try to stop a terrible fight between my parents. On that night, I saw real pain. I saw it in his blank stare. Perhaps he had accepted a pain I couldn't understand or even know.

Years later, after another horrific battle my parents had thrust upon each other and upon themselves, my father, with tears running down his face, looked me in the eyes and spoke words he would repeat several times over the years: "You don't know what I have gone through with her."

He was right, and yet we do know what we went through, my sisters and I, with both of them. After all, my parents rarely treated us as their children. We were their observers, involved in their pain, and so, in our own pain. We grew as collateral damage in their never-ending war, their never-ending need to destroy each other.

Long after we had moved away, I drove past our old house in Union, Allison and Emily in the car, nonplussed by the excursion. For me, it was gut-wrenching as we drove up the small hill, and I fully expected to see my father's dark-blue Oldsmobile, my mother's light-blue Cutlass. Even knowing that at least one other family had already lived there, I could swear I still saw a shroud of sadness over that home. I am certain we must have spent happy days there, but incredibly, I can't remember any.

CHAPTER THIRTEEN

MY EATING DISORDER: A WAY TO PUNISH MYSELF

I always wanted to look like my mother. She was stately and beautiful. Even after three children, she had a flat belly and long legs. She looked great in clothes, and she was always redesigning garments, with the help of her seamstress, moving dress collars, sleeves, adding buttons—she was so creative—to enhance her thin arms, narrow shoulders, and long neck. Living under her tutelage, my mother's mantra, "A moment to the lips, a lifetime to the hips," guided every bite I ate. Watching her navigate her conflicted relationship with her love of food, I too learned to desire being thin more than feeling satisfied.

Looking back, if blueberries and watermelon represented nature's weapons against my ability to become svelte and well-built, as my mother preached, then what chance did I have to develop a healthy relationship to food? For my mother, each and every meal was an opportunity to play a game of "This is good and this is bad." On what she called "normal days," she insisted that our family eat only "good" foods, such as protein, vegetables, and occasionally, fried rice she brought in from the Chinese restaurant. Dessert was canned fruit cocktail in low-sugar syrup with a splash of nondairy creamer. We had to save the "bad foods" for "binge days." Those days, she would bring home a half-gallon carton of ice milk (low-fat ice cream), which she could eat in its entirety in one night. Her belly distended, she would need to jump into a tub of hot water, her skin turning bright red, to warm her shivering body. We lived by declaring food "good" or "bad" and by counting every calorie, every morsel of food that went into our mouths. Her restrictions were all so laborious, her rigidity such a waste of life.

When my parents visited me at college in the late fall, they noticed that, away from my mother's watchful guidance, I had gained the Freshman 15. My father pointed out that, at my new weight, I "waddled like a duck." He even informed me that I was no longer "Itty Bitty Titty"; apparently, my fuller anatomy included my chest. Looking back, I realize these critical remarks were my father's way of acknowledging the change in me, now that I had transformed from a thin girl into a curvy young woman. Yet at the time, I felt demoralized. I wished my parents hadn't discussed the fact that I had left for college a size 4 and was now, as they said, "at least a size 6."

Until their visit, my first year at Emerson College in Boston had been a major success. I had chosen Emerson because of its reputation as one of the best schools for speech pathology. Our family only had the funds for me to attend Emerson for two years. I agreed that after my sophomore year, I would transfer to a state school so each of my sisters could have the same opportunity to attend a private college. Still, I felt Emerson was well worth the investment.

Throwing my hat into the election ring, I ran for secretary of my freshman class, and I won. Why was I so bold in my first months at college? Perhaps I felt this new home gave me the fresh start I needed, or perhaps the friendships I found myself easily forming encouraged me to explore leadership. As class secretary, I became a more active contributor to my new community and interfaced with the faculty as well as the students, hearing their concerns and bringing them to those who could help. I was even invited, along with the president, vice president, and treasurer, to the home of our class adviser for dinner. I still remember what was served: roasted meat with gravy, string beans, and whipped potatoes, and for dessert, chocolate cream pie with whipped cream. Every morsel was delicious, seasoned as it was with the knowledge that I was there! How special for a girl who always felt "less than." And soon I became "popular" on campus. I found myself dating every weekend, although I was still in like/love with my high school sweetheart, Bruce. On a work scholarship, I loved working as the receptionist at the student union, where I became well-informed about everything that was happening at our school. Even the high grades that my scholarship required me to maintain proved within my reach, since I loved what I was learning and studied hard.

Meanwhile, Bruce was attending Lehigh University, an all-male college in Bethlehem, Pennsylvania. By the time we left home for college, we had been dating for close to two years, and I had decided we needed to be free to date others. And date, I did! Even when we were both home, I rarely saw Bruce, since he was either working or playing sports. Suddenly, at Emerson the young men were all right there, and I was surprised at how they pursued me. Most of the young men who asked me out were respectful and had the potential, if I were interested, to become more of a part of my life. But any date who felt even mildly aggressive terrified me. In their defense, it was the era of the sexual revolution, but I was not evolved. I was unable to separate myself from normal expectations, seeing myself as in danger, fragile, vulnerable. It was less the physical pain that caused me so much concern. I was certain those unknown to me would hurt me emotionally, see the chinks in my armor.

Understandably, many of my dates assumed I was enjoying the freedom of the 1960s, with its interconnected drug culture and sexual revolution, but this could not have been further from the truth. I felt fearful of intimacy, even with Bruce. While I wanted to venture beyond my fear of physical closeness, I still kept him at a distance. Now that I was a young woman, the veil I had wrapped around myself as a child to protect me from feeling pain prevented me from feeling free to explore pleasure with Bruce, and certainly with those other young men as well. Having grown up with emotional abuse and neglect, I had no road map for emotional connection, and physical connection seemed to me a frightening step even further beyond what I knew.

I was, however, seduced by the simple freedom to enjoy myself. I loved to listen to poetry at tiny tables in teahouses, where I drank hot mint tea and nibbled on chocolate-chip or corn muffins fresh from the oven. Study parties included date nut bread and cream cheese, and I wanted to enjoy all of them. As I was small in stature, it didn't take long for me to put on those extra pounds. However, it was less my awareness of the weight I had gained than my awareness of the differences between my peers and me that contributed to my slide into anorexia, the first of my two eating disorders. When I saw my college friends interacting with their parents, I noticed my peers were not apologizing for something, for anything, as I still apologized to my mother and father over and over again. Instead, my friends were having conversations about school, about their classes, about what they were doing in Boston, sharing their good times. And their parents were listening with curiosity, warmth, and encouragement, bonding with their young adult children. Witnessing how my friends' parents supported their burgeoning independence, I felt more defective than ever. Every trip, Sunday dinner, and friendship with another family informed me of the contrast between my friends and me: They were treasured, and I was not. Perhaps I was wrong about my friends and their families, but I sensed they were not hiding shameful secrets. Instead, I was the one trying to hide my shameful family. My Sunday phone calls to my parents always ended with my mother crying that I didn't love her or miss her and that she couldn't believe I wasn't mourning our separation. I felt guilt every week, and ironically, years later, when I was married, I felt the same guilt every Sunday as well. She certainly never felt the need to "let me off the hook" of being responsible for her happiness.

The voice I heard inside my mind constantly reminded me that my friends deserved families who loved them and I did not. I was bad; they were good. I was a fake, living the lies of a student who deserved to be at Emerson College. I knew I deserved none of the opportunities I had received. There were nights when, falling asleep, I envisioned an angel on one side of my pillow and a devil on the other. In my mind's ear, I would hear them screaming at each other, revealing how damaged I was, how I didn't fit in, how sad and pathetic I truly was. Their voices told me it was only a matter of time before everyone who thought they knew me found out what I truly was—trash. Regardless of how many dates, good grades, or accomplishments I had, I felt less than—t-r-a-s-h!

A battle was raging within me. I was used to my father's hurtful comments about my body, so I felt I deserved them. The life I was familiar with felt desirable. My new life at college, however, had brought me so many positive experiences that I was beginning to feel a different kind of desire. I was becoming aware that there were other lives I might want, and even other lives I might actually deserve.

At Emerson, I experienced happiness for the first time. I had so many close friends who wanted to spend time with me, earned excellent grades in speech pathology—Emerson's most demanding major at the time—and received invitations to every dance, party, and hangout. Still, I questioned who I was to enjoy that happiness. Certain I was wearing the mask of someone who belonged to that happy world, I grew more and more despondent. The feeling that I was living a lie made me so miserable that by Thanksgiving I was considering not returning to Emerson after the holiday. I needed to run from all that was good and nurturing. I simply could not allow myself to partake of happiness any longer. Guilt reared its ugly head over and over again. I was in a place that provided me with safety, connection, and hope, while my sisters were trapped with my parents in the life I knew all too well. There were also whisperings my father was using his math acumen and intelligence to do some gambling and booking, and although it sounded as if he was making money, it was terribly frightening to me. I was so worried that, once again, he would be hauled off to jail. And emotionally, it sabotaged my sense of right from wrong since, although legal today, gambling wasn't legal at that time. "Do as I say, not as I do."

My frequent nightmares revealed memories I had buried deep inside myself. Each nightmare began with a scene like Picasso's *Guernica*, an explosion of somber gray, black, and white, the beginning of the dance my parents did as they gathered the impetus for their fights. Then as the nightmare turned the kaleidoscope of my unstable family life, I felt myself trapped in a fun house of mirrors always leading nowhere, clearly because nowhere was where I felt I was. Once their fights became or threatened to become violent, I was blinded by the glaringly bright colors of chaos. In my dreams, I ran from one end of a tilting tunnel to the other. Each time I arrived at either end, my friends and their families would be there, laughing at me and my family. They saw who I was, a part of a family so different from others. I could no longer pass for the person I felt I had become at Emerson.

Each night before bed, I would sort through my memories of my family like pick-up sticks. Examining each scene one by one, I would stack them together until they all fell off one another, dropping to the ground. It was too much to bear. I knew my family was diametrically opposite to the families I now saw through the eyes of my friends. Like a groundswell, all the awareness I had hidden rose over me as I laid my head upon my pillow. Then the cacophony of my mother's screeching, coupled with my father's accusations, would finally lull me into fitful sleep.

Sometimes I dreamed that Bruce was sent to Vietnam (as so many of our generation had been) and immediately killed. This nightmare grew more and more overpowering and seemingly real. Mourning him each night, I acknowledged there would be nobody to save or protect me. My fear that Bruce would go to Vietnam and never return soon became overwhelming, especially since I felt conflicted: Did I want him to save me or let me die as well? The limited self-worth I had bolstered with my happiness, excitement to learn, and active social life now teetered, and I was filled with even more guilt for desiring a new life, especially if it were away from Bruce. Looking back, in my nightmares, perhaps Bruce, who had known and accepted me for years, represented my link to my family life, which filled me with sadness but was more familiar, and possibly more comfortable, than actually feeling joy. The subconscious mind is so powerful, creating connections we sometimes cannot understand until decades later. Decades later, I now recognize that the angel and the devil, who often sat on my sheets as I climbed into bed, ready to do battle for my attention, represented my fight with myself. I loved Bruce, and that was the angelic side. But I also wanted him gone, the devilish side, so I would be assured there was never any happiness to be written into my life story, happiness I was certain I did not deserve.

That entire Thanksgiving vacation, I was terribly unsettled, feeling I had to make a decision. There came a turning point. Perhaps it was the moment, as many people say, when I chose life over death. By the end of vacation, I had discerned that my tendency to hide that which hurt so much—my guilt for leaving my sisters unprotected from my parents—had led me to run away from a life I believed I wanted. I wanted now to stay alive and grow. The silvery-winged angel who sat upon my shoulder, the shoulder so used to bearing responsibility for everyone, encouraged me to pursue my goal of becoming a speech pathologist by continuing the excellent education I was receiving at Emerson. The professors there were leaders in my chosen area of study, writing the books on speech pathology, and I was a hungry acolyte. I decided to finish my freshman year in Boston. I already knew my time there would be limited, so onward I went. I would fly or fail.

Returning to school provided the opportunity to partake even more in the independent and, I hoped, unencumbered life I desired and had already begun to create. I dug in fiercely with strength and determination, seeking to make the most of my time left in Boston. Sororities were rushing, and I was told I was a desired rush choice. I was honored to be chosen, honored that so many young women had confidence in me! My classes were challenging, and I loved the new skills I was learning. I wanted to join every club on campus, and I soon spent all of my free time in the broadcasting studio, longing to grab a microphone. Perhaps in another life, had speech pathology not been my area of study, I would have drifted toward broadcasting as a major and future career.

That winter was brutally cold and windy. My hip yellow parchment-paper earrings cut deeply into my ears, drawing blood, as I walked past the river to class on Charles Street. But I was finding my way. I loved each taste of freedom and choice, to be a young woman studying in one of the most exciting cities in the world, even when it was only snow upon my tongue.

Having found a community where I belonged, I was now a thriving member of the class, taking notes as class secretary, a potential dean's list student, everyone's friend. Yet sadly, each weekend when I called home, I heard through my conversations with my sisters or parents that, of course, the life I had left behind was still the same. My parents' fights continued, but now I assumed they fought about me and the expense of sending me to Emerson. Whenever I spoke with my family, my balloon of happy air simply dissipated, and I hung up feeling angry with myself and, once again, guilty.

How could I have been so happy while my sisters were mistreated and miserable? How could my parents end their ranting and fighting without me there to stop them or take the blame? Guilt lived in every corner of my room, in every book I read, in every class I attended. Guilt lurked around every corner, and soon it overtook my spirit, once again.

As freshman year continued, I lost my resolve. I stopped dating. Rather than socializing in the cafeteria with other students, I began eating meals by myself. That meant eating a hard-boiled egg for breakfast and a can of tuna fish and an apple for dinner. The weight fell off me, but I still felt ugly. I was enjoying myself while my sisters were suffering. What could be uglier than that? I grew listless, losing my spirit along with the weight. I felt as though a boulder were growing on my narrow shoulders.

Sophomore year brought the opportunity for me to attack myself further. I was now firmly entrenched in the eating disorder known as the starvation disease, anorexia nervosa. With the precision of a general planning an attack, I plotted my own self-punishment. Starvation was a perfect solution for a young woman with secrets to hide. Isolation calmed my ever-increasing anxiety. No food, no friends, no dates, no socializing, no joy. Starving myself felt perfectly commensurate with what I deserved. I felt such a heightened responsibility for my family's suffering that punishing myself became all that mattered to me.

My natural tendency to overachieve remained in high gear. As I starved myself, since I was on a work scholarship, I also worked two jobs, made dean's list, babysat for the children of my professors, removed my name from the Dream Girl of Sophomore Year contest for which I had been nominated, and avoided the sorority rush. The sicker I got, the sicker I got. The more I saw myself as victorious over my basic needs, the better I felt. Believe me when I say that anorexia robs a person of emotions, reactions, and reality. Like an alcoholic looking for her next drink or a drug addict searching for his next fix, an anorexic is always looking for her next way to punish herself by abstaining from food, from pleasure, from life. I was headed for self-destruction, and ready for it.

Anorexia is tantamount to gripping a tiger by the tail. *Letting go would destroy me,* I told myself. Two egg whites with mustard and black coffee became my daily allotment. When I looked in the mirror, my emaciated frame appeared huge, having nothing to do with reality. I weighed myself obsessively, all day and all night. By the end of the first semester of sophomore year, the few friends I still had were worried about me and would invite me to join them in the dining hall or at a coffee shop; however, as I continued to be "too busy" to join them, they eventually saw there was nothing they could do to help me. I felt such a need to strip myself of any pleasure that I abandoned the full social life I had once adored. I chose penance instead. Even my poor roommate moved out, since I was waking up at all hours of the night to exercise my "lazy body" and mark off on the elaborate chart I had created to keep track of every calorie eaten or burned, every two hours, how many of each exercise I had performed.

I was completely consumed by my own goal of self-destruction. The only question was how much longer I would live before totally disappearing. The amazing irony is that my eating disorder made me feel even uglier than I had felt when I gained weight. The less I ate, the more I existed on adrenaline; I aged and I felt it, but no matter—the self-flagellation felt worth it. I pursued that voice of self-hatred, always seeking a new way to punish myself, another way to degrade myself, a new way to say, *I am not worthy of food or pleasure.*

Returning home at the end of sophomore year, I knew my time in Boston had ended. Financially, it was over, so all that was left for me was resigning myself to my fate. At eighty-something pounds, I was now unrecognizable. My hair was no longer glossy and shiny, as it had once been, but wiry and stringy instead. My skin had turned from creamy white to a mottled yellowish, and I was amenorrheic, having had no period for close to ten months. My clothes hung on me, and my father cried when he first saw me. My mother called Bruce and told him to expect to see a different person than the one he had last seen. I had lost all my enthusiasm for him, and for everyone else as well. He and I broke up that summer; there had been little to keep us together for a while.

I tried to force his hand to end our relationship, but he couldn't do it. Perhaps he felt something in his psyche about a "sinking ship." Finally, I had to tell him I didn't love him anymore. In reality, I probably didn't love anyone. I had become numb to all emotions. If he was shocked or hurt, feeling unloved or abandoned, I don't know. To this day, I assume his own survival instincts must have sheltered him from those emotions, and he must have instead felt relieved to no longer have me, my boulder (the weight I carried around everywhere), and my misery, in his life.

My plan was to attend the state college in my town. I had taken the city bus in one direction to high school, and now I would take it in the other direction to the local college. Being there to protect my sisters was essential for their and my survival, I told myself, but in reality, all I was doing was giving up. The hatred I felt for myself had already overtaken me, and soon, everywhere I turned, all I could see was my own failure, my powerlessness. I began to feel a fraud. I never was anything, never would be anything, never lived that other life.

Suddenly, my survival instinct must have kicked in, and I begged my father to let me talk with a therapist.

At the end of my sophomore year at Emerson, my friends had dragged me to our psychology professor to ask for his help with what they clearly saw as my emotional problem. I refused, over and over again, to visit him but finally acquiesced. "Dr. So-and-So, I have a problem," I blurted out, although I didn't think I did. "How far along are you?" he asked. "What? Oh no, I'm a virgin! I'm not pregnant!" I yelled, running from my friends waiting outside his office. He never looked at me. He didn't see the pain in my eyes or notice how emaciated I was. Perhaps in his mind, the only problem a coed could have was an unplanned pregnancy. Little did he know that being sexually active was the furthest thing from my mind. I hated my body and would certainly not offer it to anyone!

After that experience, I never planned on asking for help again; I believed that none would ever be available for me. In those days, therapy for mental health was largely unavailable, and if it was, it was too expensive; only rich people could talk with a therapist, and clearly, no one in my family had ever gone to therapy. I reflect back on the time when my paternal grandmother gave birth to and let die baby Aaron, and the stigma of that horrific situation. How could my needs compare? The stigma would be unacceptable in our family.

But now I was losing my ability to starve myself; not eating became an impossibility. At home there were too many distractions for me to focus on my punishing regimen. Now along with my parents' arguments, I faced my newfound awareness of the disorienting reality in our home: In my family, up was down, and vice versa. Each day held the usual challenges, just as before I had left, and I fell right back into my job of dealing with the never-ending tension between my parents. Yet I felt even more untethered than I had at college. The guardsman I had become in my war against myself was failing, and I felt the tide turning. I was clearly losing control.

My poor body! Only weeks before, I had been starving myself, and now I was eating large quantities of food, making up for months and months of starvation—yet, another punishment. I was living on laxatives. My angry bowels, having adjusted to a life without food, were suddenly cramping uncontrollably, and I was falling into a chasm of despair. I felt empty, truly amorphous, as if I didn't exist. I had no drive, determination, or need to do anything. All I wanted was to fill the hole in myself, that deep, dark hole I could not reach. Starving had been easy compared to this new place where I found myself. I now suffered, and I mean suffered, from bulimia, the binging disease, and it was hell, this attempt to fill myself with the nurturing I now understood I had never received. I ate boxes of cookies, my belly swelling until I felt I would burst. Within a few months, I went from weighing in the low 80s to 130 pounds.

I weighed myself every day, and after each defeat the scale handed me, I vowed not to eat more than an egg white and black coffee. I'd last until midmorning, when I would attack whatever food was available. Every day ended with an enormous amount of junk food, consumed with huge servings of anger, guilt, and tortuous punishment. Starving had felt satisfying. Bulimia felt disgusting! I went to visit my friend Janis at college one day, and I stopped to purchase a dozen donuts. When the server asked me what kind I wanted, I stated it didn't matter, I wasn't eating them, so whatever she chose would be fine. Driving to the college little more than a half hour away, I decided to sample one. I wound up eating the entire dozen within that half hour, powdered sugar on my clothes, humiliation weighing heavily upon my chest.

As I lost control, my panic became impossible for my family to ignore, and my father had no option but to allow me to see a psychiatrist for a short while. I was prescribed large amounts of Miltown, or Meprobamate, a tranquilizer which made me listless and lethargic, exacerbating my lack of desire to awaken. Eventually, all I did was sleep. My escape or depression? Either way, it took over my life. Suddenly, I had become my father, burrowing myself under the covers of self-hatred. The thought of awakening and facing, with despair, the person I had become anchored me to my mattress, my body buried under pillows of self-sabotage.

Once the psychiatrist had adjusted my dosage to an appropriate amount, I began talk therapy, which ironically, felt frightening rather than liberating. I became obsessed with the fear that my father was going to die. He was only forty-five years old, but he had lived such a volatile life that my anxiety about losing him took over my every thought. If he left us, my sisters and I would be all alone with my mother, a woman whose rage was uncontrollable.

But there were other reasons why I became obsessed with my father dying. His affair had left a profound impact on me; I still felt rejected by his choice to give away whatever love he could siphon from the little he offered us. Now he was also gambling huge amounts of money, and bookmaking at a time when it was illegal. My mother was happy because he was making money, but I felt dirty, disgusting, and the unfamiliar emotion of anger. My parents had taught my sisters and me a strict moral code, had explained how my grandfather Max's gambling habit had robbed his family of any chance of financial security, and now once again, one of our parents was violating the very principles of right and wrong that they espoused. But along with my anger at my father came my fear that he would be caught by the police or by the group of loan sharks now in his life.

One day, when he drove to Newark to offer the don a taste of his winnings, my father brought my preteen sister Mindy along with him. I was shocked at how absurdly dangerous and reckless my father's behavior had become. How could he put my little sister at risk, leaving her in the car while he paid homage to his new "family"? What could he have been thinking? By now, he spent most of his time lying on his bed, doing his "numbers" with multiple phones ringing and ringing. He was smoking two packs of Lucky Strikes a day and eating as much as an entire pizza in one sitting. I knew his lifestyle had to be taking its toll on his health. Perhaps my simultaneous anger at him, worry about him, and anxiety about our family's safety caused me to eat myself into oblivion. I was stuffing down my rage and my fear.

And then, on a beastly hot day at the end of June, soon after Michele's high school graduation, our lives transformed. It was a Saturday morning, and my sisters' and my dresses were ready for our trip to Maryland to attend our cousin Ira's wedding. My father's suit was hanging up, and the gold watch we had given him for Father's Day just two weeks before sat on his nightstand. Suddenly, while Michele and I were talking, my mother washing up in the bathroom adjacent to the bedroom, he dropped on the bed. Dead. It happened swiftly. While hopefully it was painless for him, his sudden death remained very painful for those of us he left behind. We knew he was dead, but the reality was beyond our comprehension. We called for emergency help, but sadly, all that was to be done was to wait for the family doctor to declare him dead.

Six hours later, our doctor arrived, having finished his office hours. My uncles, the same uncles responsible for beating my father a decade before, must have called the funeral home transport, who carried my father's body down the stairs: *thump, thump, thump.* My mother screamed and screamed, taking up all the oxygen in every room she entered. Unable to soothe her, my sisters and I watched her fall apart. Ironically, the one person with whom she had fought the most throughout her life, my grandmother Gittel, stayed with my mother, sleeping in her bed, giving my mother a place to rest her head. I remember assuming that just as swiftly as we had lost my father, we would soon lose my mother. For weeks I was on tenterhooks, ready to cope with her death, which did not come. Instead, as volatile and self-absorbed as she had always been, she was now even angrier and even more filled with self-pity.

Widowed at forty-two, with three daughters, my mother was incapable of carrying on. We all tried to hold her together, but she was inconsolable. At the funeral, she immediately fainted. My uncle revived her with a pocketful of smelling salts, perhaps provided by the funeral staff. But she looked as if she would faint again. The scene at my father's funeral exemplified her inability to see beyond herself: As her siblings, our aunts and uncles, held her up, my mother seemed oblivious to the three young daughters holding one another, sitting on the other side of the chapel. She made her sentiment clear. She had lost her husband; we had only lost our father. That became her dictum, over and over again. I often wonder if it was my mother's mantra that prevented me from fully mourning my father during that time or if it was my own digging in my heels, telling myself that grieving was useless, just as so many of my emotions had been. As before his death, down was up, and up was down in our family. Recently, I asked my therapist to help me grieve my father after over fifty years. There was still so much guilt around my inability to feel his death. She told me I *have* grieved him, each and every day. Perhaps ....

My last memory of the cemetery, as I took in the image of the workers shoveling dirt upon my father's casket, was of several black cars just idling on the road with their occupants standing outside them. These men, wearing black suits on this beastly hot day, stood together, appearing to chat. But their eyes were glued to us, to our family, as we walked to the car that was taking us home. It wasn't until one of my father's bookie cronies identified them for us that I realized these men were the loan sharks, watching to be certain my father was truly dead; he must have owed them money. For weeks I lived in fear that they would come to our door to collect, guns drawn, but nobody ever did.

At the shiva, I sat stone-faced, unable to believe this was our reality, our new life, a life without my father. My uncle approached me on the first night and scolded me, "From now on, you have to be a good girl. No more therapy; it is too expensive. You are to stop this nonsense with eating and not eating. Just eat!" If only it were that easy! During the week of shiva, eating every piece of Danish that arrived in the kitchen, I gained five more pounds. As we left our home at the end of shiva to walk the block and begin anew, I felt myself waddling out the front door "like a duck," as my father had said.

That night, my mother came into my room and yelled, "You killed your father! If you were only normal, and ate normally, and didn't cry, he would still be alive!" I would take that message and internalize it, along with any other accusation she could throw at me. I felt as lost as I could ever imagine being, deserving to be tossed from her graces. It would take years, and a great deal more therapy, for me to forgive myself. My mother never did.

Today I recognize that my mother wanted to blame someone for her pain, but even more so, she viewed reality through a distorted lens. While I was willing to own any blame she (or many others, for that matter) threw at me, I was ultimately powerless to have caused my father's heart attack or stroke; his lifestyle and genetics were responsible for that. Yet back then, I accepted the new shame and guilt my mother added to the boulder I carried on my shoulders; her reality weighed me down with even more self-hatred.

Bruce was gone from my life, albeit by my sending him away. His mother wrote to him while he was at basic training with the National Guard in Fort Polk, Louisiana, and he sent our family a sympathy card, signed, "With love, Bruce." It was the right thing, the only thing to do, but I needed so much more from him, and from everyone in my life. Fortunately, my sisters had boys in their lives to soften their pain.

My mother, unable to cope with her new life as a widow, left us and lived with my aunt and uncle that summer. They nurtured and supported her. Meanwhile, my sisters and I were together at home, taking care of ourselves and one another. We were still so young; I was twenty, Michele seventeen, and Mindy fourteen. Michele did all the cooking; I paid the bills, although I have no memory of where I had the funds to do so. We tried to take care of Mindy, but we worked at a jewelry store and were gone most of the day.

Eventually, toward the end of the summer, my mother returned, but she was still unable to face her new life, accept my father's death, or forgive me. I felt alone with my mother's rejection, truly alone. Boxes of cookies and candy became my only comfort.

Years of exploring my feelings in talk therapy, modifying my behaviors, taking medication, and learning to soothe myself in healthy ways have finally brought me to a place of acceptance and forgiveness for what I did to my body during those years. I do not have answers for these eating disorders. They are terribly difficult, the living with and the treatment for. I suppose all my healing led to this: I became ready to find myself, to be kinder to myself, to no longer need food to nurture myself, no longer need food to punish myself, no longer need to starve myself. I was ready to love myself.

CHAPTER FOURTEEN
GETTING MARRIED

Saturday, June 28, 1969, was the day my father died at forty-five years old. He died of a massive heart attack or stroke; in deference to Jewish laws, there was no autopsy, so we are unsure of the exact cause. It was sudden and hopefully free of pain or awareness.

Friday, June 28, 1970, was the night of my surprise bridal shower—all the more surprising because, as intuitive as I was, I never thought anyone would throw me a shower on the first anniversary of my father's death. I was still mourning.

Awakening on the morning of my shower, I carefully laid my clothes on my bed; I was thinking past work to the evening. Bruce had told me we were dining at a restaurant in East Orange, so I dressed in a lavender "leather" wrap skirt, a pink-and-lavender blouse, and iridescent pumps with a multicolor handbag. My hair was freshly washed, and my makeup kept with the color scheme: lavender eyes and a soft-pink mouth. My marquise diamond engagement ring had been freshly cleaned at the jewelry store where my sisters and I worked during college. I was always excited to have a date night with Bruce, and I knew that tonight he would hold me a bit tighter to assuage my sadness at the solemn reminder of losing my father.

This may be a good time to explain how Bruce and I found our way back to each other after our estrangement. That fateful summer of 1969 had been one of growth for me, despite the death of my father and my family's struggles to adjust to our new lives as a group of four women. As my mother was traveling back and forth to and from her sister's home, and my sisters had their boyfriends to confide in, I began to write poetry to assuage my loneliness. Writing was healing; the daily exercise of poetry helped me not only face the deeply hidden parts of myself, my anger, shame, and fear, but also find my optimism and spirit. Each day, before and after work, I would write—some poems flowery and soft, some dark and moody, and some hopeful. Each one ended with thoughts of the love I had for Bruce and how much I wished he were in my heart again.

Grounded by my poetry, I wrote to Bruce in basic training and suggested we talk when he returned to New Jersey; I was open to it. I also shared that I had done a great deal of work on myself. I didn't tell him I had been healing from bulimia. My eating disorder, not yet totally gone, was now becoming less and less present. As I filled the pages of my notebooks with my words, I ameliorated the need to fill my soul with food. I felt myself moving away from the compulsion to punish myself.

Affairs of the heart are so surprising. I assumed Bruce and I would meet and talk, he would remain stoic, having been hurt by my ending our relationship, and it would take time for him to trust me if we were to see each other again. But when we met, Bruce didn't seem to see an Ellyn (significantly) heavier and more tearful than the one who had left him. Instead, he saw a woman who had weathered yet another storm in life and survived. He wanted to see me again, and again, and within a month, we were engaged. My mother was the only one who didn't smile when she saw my ring. Of course, Bruce had already asked her permission to marry me; that condition was nonnegotiable, as I knew I would pay a steep price if he did not ask her first. But my mother had no desire to see me leave her, even as she had no interest in being with me.

Bruce picked me up for our date, and as we walked into the restaurant, I felt a momentary rush: I thought I saw familiar faces through the glass doors. But that would be impossible. Nobody would throw a party for me on the first anniversary of the death of my father. Besides, I wasn't getting married for two more months; there was still plenty of time to organize a wedding shower.

Suddenly, from all corners, the room of close to one hundred women exploded with shouts of "Surprise!" All around me were my friends, my family, the friends of my in-laws, and a few of my mother's friends too. I began to cry—actually, to sob. I felt a combination of shock, excitement, and memories of my father lying dead on his bed flooding through me. It took me a while to calm down and enjoy the fact that all of these women were there for me. I was overwhelmed by the generosity of my Aunt Shirley, who had offered a home to my mother over that past year and now had organized this shower for me. I hugged her, my mother, and my mother-in-law, Eleanor. I felt my heart pounding in my chest.

Bruce told me that he and Michele's fiancé, Ira, would be back later. (Michele and Ira had been dating for a few years. He was wonderful in supporting us as we grieved my father's death, and Michele and Ira got engaged soon after Bruce and I; their wedding would be the following June.) I began to circulate among the guests, thanking everyone for attending. The night flew by, and I felt like a princess, opening gifts and receiving so many "best of luck" and "see you at the wedding" wishes.

By the end of the shower, my mother's smile seemed to indicate that she too was elated to have received so many congratulations on my pending marriage. Yet when she looked at me, she seemed distant and cold. I sensed her transformation, even when she pretended to be happy for me. I knew she was angry. I just didn't know my transgression—yet.

I must have thanked my mother and my aunt for the wonderful shower ten times each. Meanwhile, my belly was growing distended with pain, a physical manifestation of my fear that I had angered my mother. With my usual self-flagellation, I asked myself over and over, *What did I do wrong? Was I not warm enough? Did I not hug her enough? Did I not compliment her on her outfit, her hair?* Knowing how important her appearance was to her, I always made sure to give her compliments. Maybe I hadn't given her enough for such a big event. Had I not soothed her, praised her, shown her enough gratitude? Somehow, I had failed her.

Then Bruce and Ira returned to help cart all the wonderful gifts to our home. Guests were leaving the shower with hugs and kisses. I still remember the parting words of several guests who told me they loved how excited and enthusiastic I was to be a future bride and were looking forward to seeing me walk down the aisle.

Bruce, Ira, Michele, and I loaded the gifts into the car and station wagon and headed to our home. When we arrived, we brought the dozens of gifts into our family room. We carefully placed them on the floor and sofa. Then Michele and I kissed our guys good night. It was time to get ready for bed; we both had work the next day and were exhausted.

No sooner did the door close than my mother came racing down the stairs, screaming. "How could you enjoy yourself tonight when your father is lying in the ground, dying a year ago today? How could you?" Then her talons emerged. She gripped my arm and slapped my face until welts emerged on my skin. "Get those gifts out of this house, or I will throw them in the garbage! If they are here in the morning, you will never see them again, and I mean it!"

I knew she meant it. There was no discussing anything with her when she was in that state. I had seen this transformation before, and I knew her body was filled with adrenaline, the same adrenaline she had used to pull my sisters and me from our sleep to clean the kitchen or fulfill whatever need she felt at that moment. She was wild, and we wanted to be anywhere but there with her.

Taking our mother at her word, Michele and I knew there was nothing to be done but move the gifts. Bruce and Ira returned with the car and station wagon. We reloaded every gift back in, and the guys caravanned to the home of my future in-laws. The gifts—Tuscany by Lenox dishes and serving pieces, Grande Baroque by Wallace flatware, pots, pans, an ironing board and iron, and on and on—which I had treasured just a few hours ago had now become terrible problems for me. Part of me never wanted to see them again, as I felt I had sold my soul for china and silver. But then again, I reminded myself, my mother's most recent attack of blame and shame was in keeping with her typical patterns throughout my life. She would not allow my positive experiences to remain happy ones, not now, at this important moment in my life, not ever!

When Bruce told her there was no room in my home for the bounty, my future mother-in-law cleared the Ping-Pong table in her basement. Bruce was now protecting my mother the same way I did, by carefully hiding the truth about her behavior. I know he did it for me, but I don't think Bruce wanted his parents to find out more about my mother's behavior either.

The next morning, Michele and I were dressed for work and preparing our breakfast when my mother, wild-eyed, came running down the stairs into the family room. "Where are the gifts?" she demanded. "I never saw them at the shower! Where are they? What did you do with them?" I informed her they were at my future in-laws'. "You didn't even let me see them! I don't matter to you at all, do I? I am only your mother, but I know you love your mother-in-law more!"

Certainly, this wasn't the first time my mother had distorted reality. Still, I felt shocked and terrified. As calmly as I could, I reminded her that the night before, she had wanted the gifts out of the house, so they were now at the home of my future in-laws, the logical place for them.

"What? You mean to tell me that they get to have the gifts, and I don't get to even see them? You are so ungrateful, so selfish, having a beautiful shower on the night your father died one year ago to the day, and I don't even get to see your gifts?" She bared her teeth.

Michele and I ran out the door and drove to work. I tried to stop shaking. My face was swollen from tears and bruises. Rather than a future bride with beautiful memories of a beautiful shower, I was a mess. Sadly, I must admit that at that time, I felt I deserved my mother's attacks. It was easier to believe her than indulge myself in the fantasy that I was worthy of more than my mother had ever given me. Even with all the work I had done on myself to heal my eating disorder, the outward evidence of my self-loathing, I still had a lot more to learn and accept about myself and my family. It would take decades for me to see how severely my mother had hurt, and how severely she had hurt me, and how unfair her treatment of me truly was. Perhaps the feeling that my mother had wronged me, and that I had deserved better, fully came together for me as I celebrated the engagements and weddings of my daughters with joy, the unabashed joy Bruce and I felt for them and their husbands. Today I can think of nothing Bruce and I wouldn't do to make our children and their partners happy.

I was still in shock. Fortunately, one of the ladies who worked with me at the store applied concealer to my bruises; I am certain she was wondering what had happened to me. A few hours later, my boss told me I had a phone call from Eleanor. Answering, I heard a cold response at the other end of the phone. I was surprised; she had always been warm and loving to me.

"Ellyn, this is Eleanor Mantell, and I am very surprised at what I have learned this morning from your mother. The poor lady, your mother, never got to see your shower gifts, and she called me sobbing. How could you treat her that way? I have invited her to come to lunch and see the gifts in the basement, and I think you should come here to make her feel better. And I am very surprised at you for your lack of consideration for what she has been through. I hope you will never treat me that way."

I was speechless at my mother's ability to paint herself as the victim. How could she have lied about me to Eleanor? How could I face my soon-to-be mother-in-law again?

I didn't defend myself. I told Eleanor I could not leave work but was terribly sorry to have hurt my mother. It had been thoughtless of me to take the gifts from my house before she could see them. I vowed never to treat Eleanor in such a hurtful way and stated that I was very remorseful for my actions. Then I hung up and ran to the bathroom. I was not sure whether I was about to cry or vomit.

Why did I lie rather than speak the truth? Because that was what I did—anything to protect my mother and her delusions from the consequences of reality. How can I explain that my tie to her was so strong that lying was only one of the many things, regardless of how wrong, I would have done for her? If my sisters and I had learned anything in order to survive, it was that if our mother fell apart, we would all fall apart. So strong was our need to hold her up, to keep her standing.

The two months between my shower and our wedding were brutal. My mother seethed, unable to make peace with my marrying, bonding to a husband who came from a loving family, one willing to embrace me. The closer my mother and I came to separating, the angrier and more physically volatile she became. Every opportunity she had, she would remind me that I was leaving and she was alone, despite my two sisters remaining with her. She took my marriage as a personal attack. Her teeth and talons were always at the ready. She seized every opportunity she had to grab and pinch at me. I tried to avoid her, but suddenly, she was everywhere I walked in our home, claws out.

Our wedding was scheduled for late August, but I begged Bruce to elope every time we were together. July was a month of turmoil for us; I felt beaten, helpless, and hopeless. But Bruce remained steadfast in rejecting my desire to cancel the wedding that was causing my mother to spiral out of control. He felt it would be unfair to elope, as our parents would not be able to see us marry and we would regret that decision forever. He was right. Consistent with my mother's mantra, "A moment to the lips, a lifetime to the hips," eloping would have felt good to me at the time, but we would wish we hadn't afterward. I was defenseless with my mother, and Bruce knew it. Yet his strong convictions told him we had to stay the course. So the weeks passed until our wedding.

On my wedding day, my sisters and I drove nearly an hour to pick up my dress. There was no air conditioning in the car on a rainy and humid day, and all three of us, along with my dress, wilted on the way back home.

Like so much surrounding my wedding, the dress caused misery for my mother and me. Months before, we had invited Eleanor to accompany us as we shopped for my wedding gown. Since my mother was tall and blonde, and Eleanor petite and dark like me, the sales consultant mistook Eleanor for the mother of the bride. Immediately, knowing how sensitive my mother was, I corrected the sales consultant, as did Eleanor, but the harm had already been done. The sales consultant's remark had minimized my mother, who remained inflamed no matter how much I tried to soothe her.

The gown the three of us chose was a sample, less expensive than others in the bridal shop but little the worse for wear. It had been nipped and tucked, but the sales consultant told me that once it was altered and cleaned, it would look good as new. I was so excited. It was beautiful, white as snow, with a bell-shaped satin body and sleeves and a high lace neck. Once the consultant had added the Juliet headpiece and attached the veil, I became a bride! Thrilled, I kissed my mother. I imagined myself carrying a spray of flowers and wearing a smile and a glow I knew would come from the center of my being as I walked down the aisle to meet Bruce. I felt like royalty in the gown and couldn't wait for Bruce to see me in it.

But my joy in my wedding dress became tainted by my mother's insecurity. She still felt her status had been diminished by the saleswoman's unintentional insult. When we returned home, my mother reminded me that she had raised me, had stayed up at night with me when I was sick. Who was Eleanor to be treated as the "mother"? I had long since given up on reasoning with my mother when she felt insulted or sorry for herself.

As punishment, my mother added that she would never allow the dress in the house; she threatened to cut it up if I disobeyed her. She told me I would have to pick up the dress on the day of my wedding and bring it to the banquet hall. I agreed to whatever demands she made; she was, as always, in charge. As she said, while I was living in her home, I would follow her rules. Otherwise, I would make her angry and unhappy, which I did anyway, even when I cooperated.

The night before my wedding, my dress was still in the store waiting for me. On that night, my mother's tirade proved impressive, even for her. As she had every day, she blamed me for my father's death. Had I not had an eating disorder, he would be here now. Had I not had emotional problems, he would not have had stress. Had I been a more loving daughter, had I not done this, or that …. Finally, she concluded that, had I only done this or that, he would still be alive to walk her down the aisle. Not me, her! It never occurred to her that I was being given away to Bruce by my uncle, the very one I saw beat my father years ago! Sadly, I accepted it all, all of the remorse and the responsibility for everything that had killed my father. I believed whatever she threw at me. I knew she would attack me physically next. Knowing how easily I bruised, I begged her not to hit my face. "Please, Mommy, I want to look my best at my wedding." At that, she went to her room, slammed the door, and spent my last night at home in her own lonely world. What made this tirade so sad was the way it disconnected us. Had she only given me one instant of acceptance and happiness for falling in love and preparing to marry, we could have spent that last night in our home as mother and daughter, but instead, she must have cried herself to sleep, just as I did in the other bedroom.

The next morning, while my sisters and I were driving to pick up my dress, my mother was having her hair and nails done. None of the Finkel sisters had the opportunity to prepare for the wedding as she did. But we vowed on that day, as on so many others, that we would support one another, even if my mother couldn't. "The dress," as it became known, was soon altered, realtered, and worn by both of my sisters at their weddings. We helped one another dress, apply makeup, and prepare to become brides the way one should with the people who love her. In sharing the dress, my sisters and I anointed ourselves one another's surrogate mothers, openly giving each other succor and support in times of transition and celebrating our love as true mothers do at the most wonderful times of their daughters' lives.

We didn't need our hair or nails done for my wedding because, as usual, it was, in fact, my mother's day. With her hair perfectly coiffed and her nails shining red, my mother, wearing a stunning white dress with brown embroidery, walked down the aisle alone, unwilling to be escorted by one of her brothers or friends. She wanted to send a clear message: She was widowed, miserable, and now losing her daughter, the one she blamed for the death of her husband. Nobody had any doubt, I am certain, that she was in agony. Her eyes were turned down, staring at the carpet as if there were bread crumbs she needed to follow to get to the chuppah. The grimace on her face told everyone she was in mourning, suffering, trying her best to survive. She could not find a way to smile.

Sadly, the day my sisters and I cleaned out my mother's house, decades later, I found the dress my sisters and I had worn with such love for one another thrown in the back of the crawl space. It was disgustingly dirty and stained, covered in animal droppings, tossed aside like trash. In contrast to my own mother, after each of my daughters married, I cleaned her wedding gown and stored it in a keepsake box, a treasure for each daughter to remember the love she has for her husband, and the love my husband and I have for her.

CHAPTER FIFTEEN
FEAR OF THE RABBIT HOLE: MOTHERHOOD

By the time I was ready to become a mother, I was well aware of my fear that I would become *my* mother. Her behaviors had terrified me as a child: her constant inconsistency, volatility and unpredictability, rage and anger, night raids and manipulations. I could not, would not, bring into this world a child who would feel about me as I, sadly, felt about my mother. As Elizabeth Barrett Browning famously wrote, "How do I love thee / Let me count the ways / Love me *more*!" My mother needed us, her children, to enumerate our list of undying devotion to and adoration of her every hour of every day. I had no idea why my mother behaved as she did, only that she wanted the three of us to love her more than anything in the world, even as she made us feel inadequate, trapped, and in a state of constant confusion. We knew that if she could take our oxygen, she would do it, so in need was she of owning us, body and soul, her own survival most important to her. She radiated unceasing demands: *Save me, take care of me, love me, never leave me.* Followed soon thereafter by *I HATE YOU!* We could never fulfill her need for us, her children, to mother *her*; it was all too much for us to bear. I believe we all felt a failure at every turn, unable to assuage her unhappiness as she looked at us with her sad and troubled eyes.

In my twenties, my therapist identified my mother as having "schizoid tendencies" and did her best to try to separate the behaviors from the person. "You love your mother, but don't like her behavior, her moods, her tirades, her actions. When you are a mother, how will you be different?" my therapist wanted to know. I wanted to know as well. My fear that my child would fear me felt untenable. I was sickened with the thought that I would terrorize my child. I knew I had work to do to prepare for the decision to become a mother. I would need to start by anticipating how my family would look. The problem is that it is virtually impossible to anticipate how one will mother, and it is totally impossible when one has been mothered by a mother with mental illness.

Today, as the field of mental health has advanced, I have gained deeper insights into my mother. Conversations with mental health professionals suggest that my mother's behavior aligned more closely with borderline personality disorder than with schizophrenia. Those with borderline personality disorder are said to live between reality and fantasy, and they are unable to tell or, sometimes, accept the difference. My childhood home was a borderland where reality felt like a seesaw, up one minute, down the next.

But in the 1970s, the general population knew little about mental illness, and the stigma around discussing it was enormous. As I contemplated motherhood, I knew I had been raised by not just one but two parents with differing but equally denigrating sadistic behaviors, as well as behaviors I believed only those who were mentally ill would exhibit. Now it is clear to me that my parents couldn't give us what they didn't have: stability, acceptance, the ability to share joy and calm fears. Back then I lived with shame and guilt, ruminating on whether I would be the same as my parents and whether my children would live the same life I had. I needed to know: Was I mentally ill? So entrenched in my own pain had I been, exquisite pain from lack of self-worth, that I knew I could not transfer that to my child. It simply wasn't fair!

Seeking the truth about who I was, I decided to visit a psychiatrist to better evaluate my mental health. If I were mentally unwell, having children might be a choice I was unwilling to make, particularly if no treatments were available, and Bruce and I would have to consider that choice very carefully. I was in need of knowing if the overwhelming anxiety I experienced for most of my life was considered pathological. This second opinion on my mental health was invaluable. In our consultation, he deemed me mentally well but, clearly, profoundly affected by my parents' behavior. He advised me that if I truly wanted to have children, I should recognize that the path ahead would bring great challenges. He encouraged me to find role models and harness the strengths I admired in them to navigate the challenges I would face as a mother. "Look at other women who mother with enjoyment and pleasure, are loving and caring." I found these role models in my friends—and in my mother-in-law. "Mom," as I call her, seemed to me a study in perfection and radiance. She looked complete at any time of day or night. Having grown up in chaos, I felt compelled not only by her always-impeccable appearance but also by her orderliness and predictability and her attitude of concern for everything in her world. In her home, forks, knives, and spoons actually had their own places on the table, dishes were to be washed and put away, and jars were to be cleaned after use before returning to the refrigerator. Her home was organized and neat, and although she aspired to perfection at all times, that need certainly felt more inviting than my mother's helter-skelter behavior. She openly embraced me, showed interest in me and others, did not need to be told over and over again how much I appreciated her love and kindness. She had many friends, seemed to navigate the world with little effort, and wanted to continue to grow as an adult, something I valued even at a young age. Our almost-daily conversations revolved around events around the world, society, even fashion and lighthearted happenings. Holidays were important to her, and she always included my family as part of her own, something that felt endearing. She told me she loved me as a daughter, not a daughter-in-law, and that I was a welcome addition to the family. I felt "home" with her, and if I could emulate even a portion of those qualities, I felt I could be a good mom.

My friends, particularly my friend Sharon, showed me how genuinely happy they were to be mothers. I knew that came from a place of pride and deep love for their babies. They glowed when talking with them, even as the babies just stared back with adoration. They mastered what they could and did their best when necessary. They were responsible and had gained a maturity I admired. I felt, again, if I could emulate even a portion of those qualities, I would be a good mom. I had no doubt there was so much love stored in my heart for new life. As a speech therapist, I knew my adoration for children was a true part of me, so putting together all of the elements, I began to see myself as capable of bringing a child into the world.

I had been married for three years, and many of our friends had already become parents. Suddenly, having made the important decision to have a child, all I could think about was becoming a mother. Meanwhile, Bruce was in law school while simultaneously working toward his CPA accreditation, and I was obtaining my master's degree in speech and language pathology while working in schools as a speech therapist. "We will think about starting a family after I sit for the bar exam," Bruce often reiterated, much to my frustration. I was worried I might lose my nerve. But he wanted to ensure he had established his career before becoming a father. I had fallen in love with Bruce for so many reasons, not the least of which were his pragmatism and stability. Still, I wanted to join my friends with growing bellies and feel all of the excitement they were experiencing myself.

I soon recognized that I was better at taking my life one step at a time rather than acting on the pressure I felt to prove I was different from my own mother. I put on the brakes until Bruce sat for the bar exam on July 25 and 26, 1973, and on April 24, 1974, our beautiful Allison Beth arrived right on her due date. As much as my body had been preparing for her arrival, I still felt unprepared for that moment. Suddenly, Allison was not only my daughter, she was mine to protect, guide, and most importantly, nurture so that she could grow to love her life. I wanted her to reach her full potential, to be loved fully and unconditionally. But she was a gift, and I was unfamiliar with receiving gifts without my own mother's criticism attached.

Soon, rather than feeling the joy of becoming a mother to my own child, I began having nightmares as I relived the overwhelming anxiety I had felt as a young child taking on my own mother's responsibilities. I loved Michele and Mindy with my entire being, but I had been too young to parent them when I was still a child myself. I had functioned with a half-developed brain when "raising" Michele, who then "raised" Mindy. Remembering the challenges I had experienced, my now-developed brain was questioning my ability to be the real mother my daughter deserved.

I felt paralyzed with fear that I would fail to protect Allison, that I would hurt my captivating child, but then, when I put her to my breast and nuzzled her damp head, something kicked in: It was another gift, the guidance of my own instincts. I realized I did not need anyone to tell me how to love my gorgeous child. I would treasure her, and together, we would find our way. I began to trust myself; my inner voice would respond to Allison, and we would build a life together. I now understood that I had not been genetically programmed to become my mother. I was genetically programmed to love unconditionally, to learn alongside so many other women, and to provide stability and comfort for my daughter. I would sleep at night knowing that I had done everything I could to help her to grow in every way I had been afraid to grow as a child.

My mother had made it abundantly clear to me that I was never loving enough, never able to cover her with the blanket of undying gratitude for her every action. She had expected my sisters and me to shower her with praise and kneel before her for penance if we did not. She would settle for nothing less than our apologizing over and over for every transgression she perceived us to have committed. We were privy to how hard she worked to provide a home for us. We owed our undying appreciation to her, no matter what distorted perception kept her mind fixated on our crimes against her. Would I repeat the accusations, entitlement, and contempt that had shaped my vision of motherhood? My mother's derision made me feel that I had failed at being a daughter. Now would I also fail at being the mother Allison needed?

Despite my understanding of the influence of my past on my present, as a young mother, I faced a draining, frightening battle between self-trust and self-doubt, and Allison's well-being stood in the balance. Many nights, my nightmares paralleled those I had experienced in college, as I ran through the mirrored fun house that always led me further and further away from peace. This time, I was holding a baby to my leaking breast and unable to find diapers for her. I berated myself for not knowing how to care for this precious gift. My daughter, with her darkest hair and big black-brown eyes, her kissy lips and rosy skin, deserved more than a mother who simply adored her. She deserved a mother who felt confident in her ability to provide stability, who would nurture her abundantly rather than remaining paralyzed by her own pain. My greatest desire was for my daughter to love herself, but I had never been capable of loving myself.

I returned to watching the women who would provide a road map for me, as my own mother had not. Allison deserved nothing less. My mentors saved me, and Allison, from my feelings of helplessness, something they had no idea they were doing for both of us. Yet unfortunately, the more I saw my models excelling in raising their children, the worse I felt about myself. The loving language they spoke seemed to come from a natural place, whereas I thought excruciatingly hard about every word I said to my baby, so frightened I would scar her if I said something wrong. As I second-guessed my every action, I lost what little confidence I had in my ability to rise to the enormous task I had set in front of myself. As I compared myself to the mothers I viewed as standards of perfection, everything that seemed to come naturally to these women seemed unattainable for me. At what age should I be reading books to Allison? At what point should I be taking her to the park? "Better mothers" seemed to know these things that were elusive to me. I did, however, recognize that I had one superpower: an energy that propelled me forward. I was always hungry for evolution and growth. My overwhelming desire to better myself made me commit fully to creating a family far healthier than the one that had raised me.

When the nightmares became more imposing—dropping Allison as I carried her, forgetting her in the car, not taking her to the doctor when she was sick—I knew it was time for me to reach out to a professional once again. By now, she was about nine months old, and her world was getting bigger as she crawled everywhere. But I faced obstacles in accessing help. Bruce was not on board, fearing, I believe, that therapy for a married woman meant I was unhappy with him. Even with his front-row seat to the childhood and adulthood I had survived, he worried about where therapy would lead me and whether it would impact our marriage. Bruce liked the status quo and saw no reason to change it. He was working constantly, building his career, distinguishing himself in his field. He was feeling success every day. Meanwhile, I felt I was teetering dangerously close to whatever the edge might be. This constant worry that I was enough of a mother lowered my self-worth to the point that I felt of such little value, I knew I was approaching a dangerous plateau.

Additionally, both Bruce and I felt concerned about the cost of therapy, an unexpected expense that would stress our budget. Since I felt of so little value, I couldn't bring myself to challenge the holder of our economic future, putting forth so much effort to save for the house we hoped to buy, the lifestyle we wanted to provide for our family. Eventually I screamed to Bruce that I needed help; there was no other choice. I felt myself drowning and knew I was out of options. I told Bruce that if I were to succeed in raising our beautiful daughter, I needed a life raft, and he was going to have to support me. As I advocated not only for myself but also for my family, my back became a bit straighter, and I grew stronger; I had taken my first difficult step toward caring for myself as a mother and thereby protecting my own family.

It turned out that I qualified for financial aid through Jewish Family Services, and so the cost of each therapy session would be minimal. Now that the cost had been ameliorated, it was time for me to begin the work necessary to pull myself out of the decaying rubble under which I was buried. But where to begin? So much of my life had been filled with emotional degradation and shame. I felt tainted by my life with my parents, inadequate and unworthy of care. Fortunately, my career as a speech therapist did give me a sense of pride, and Allison was a joy: bright, sweet, verbal, and engaging. I had struck it rich with her. I sewed matching clothes for us and was happiest when my days began with her kisses. As my days ended with her bath-scented hugs, I was in paradise, simply enjoying her beyond what I had felt possible.

As Bruce continued to spend more and more time at his practice, however, I was also feeling lonely. Often, I was alone. Bruce and I had Saturday nights and a portion of Sundays together, but the stimulating work he was doing consumed the rest of his week. Even while I worked through my self-hatred in therapy, I became gripped with fear that I was sliding down the rabbit hole of self-doubt from which I had climbed so hard to escape. I was back to second-guessing myself, feeling unworthy of Bruce's love and attention, and angry that I was raising Allison alone, without him. As I continued therapy, I sought to find my voice, my inner voice who would call out my needs. In order to begin to feel and communicate those needs, I had to dig even more deeply than ever before into my own pain as a survivor of trauma.

As I made progress toward accepting, loving, and asserting myself, Bruce and I decided that it was time for us to have our second child. Allison would be three when our second daughter arrived, and our new home was already very busy: Bruce was working constantly, Alli was a toddler with her own schedule of preschool and playdates with friends, and I was building my own career. I barely remember being pregnant, but when Emily Brooke arrived, our family felt complete. Emily had a crown of golden curls and hazel-gray eyes, and her skin was pale like mine. Right away, Allison loved being Emily's big sister as much as I loved being Emily's mother.

Emily arrived with a unique set of needs. She was born with a vertebral anomaly that prevented her from holding her neck erect. When the doctor recommended strengthening Emily's neck muscles, Allison became her "physical therapist," running from one end of the room to the other as Emily stretched to watch the big sister she idolized. Allison would also "read" her favorite books she had memorized to Emily as I nursed her, cementing the bond among all three of us.

The difference in Emily's neck turned out to be a symptom of Klip-pel-Feil syndrome, a lifelong challenge. She has mastered this challenge with her uncanny ability to reach every goal she has set for herself, and more. Bruce and I consider ourselves fortunate that we didn't know the extent of her disability when she was young. If we had, our anxiety would have probably caused us to put Bubble Wrap around her, prevent her from playing sports, and overprotect her from life.

Upon reflection, I admit that when Emily was an infant, I was terrified of my ability to mother her, as I worried she would never hold her head erect or meet other developmental milestones. What existed in my arsenal of weapons to protect this child whom I adored with all my heart? And how could I ever be enough for her? I learned more therapy techniques, including the Doman-Delacato method of psychomotor patterning. These helped Emily's physical development, albeit a bit delayed. She pushed herself with all of her determination, and we were there, holding her hand, every step of the way. As Emily grew, she not only faced serious challenges with her cervical spine but also learning challenges concomitant with Klippel-Feil syndrome. When she received this diagnosis, she felt broken, and I committed to giving her everything possible to help her push through that horrible pall. Emily has gone on to excel. I often say that she is my greatest accomplishment because I never stopped believing in her, and she picked up that belief in herself as she grew, reaching for and achieving more than I would have ever felt possible.

At one point, Emily received therapy for her learning disability, training for visual acuity, and emotional support for all she had on her plate, but she and I never gave up, and Allison was always involved in everything Emily was learning, sharing as if she were a little therapist, congratulating her on her achievements. I watched to make sure that Allison would never feel overly responsible for Emily in the ways I had felt responsible for my sisters when I was a child. I never wanted her to feel she had to anticipate all of her sister's needs and provide for their sustenance. I never wanted Allison to fear that if she could not fill these needs, her sister would perish. "Please watch Emily and let me know if she needs me" was my message, and Allison always loved to help me support her sister.

To this day, they are the best of friends, raising their families in the same community, traveling together, and caring for each other. Often, I think about my part in their friendship and know, for certain, that I intuitively met their individual needs, giving uniquely to each of my daughters, helping them to develop their personalities and strengths. A natural cheerleader, I buoyed my girls. My girls! They were beautiful children, and they are beautiful women. Allison is a school social worker and educational consultant, married to Dave, an attorney with a large financial institution. They are the loving parents of two of our grandchildren, Jake and Jessie, both in college. Emily is an entrepreneur in Human Resources, married to Jeremy, who works in finance for a large bank. They are the loving parents of Maddie, in college, and Max, in high school. They are contributors to their community. My cup runneth over!

As time passed and our children grew, we faced countless challenges, as all families do. I continued to work while raising Allison and Emily, despite the sideways glances I received from many women who thought it shameful that a woman who "didn't have to work" did so. Bruce made it clear, and I knew it to be true, that I had a good education and should contribute to the family earnings. Furthermore, in my mind, I did have to work. I needed each and every day to prove I deserved to be—to be a mother, to be a wife, to be a sister, to be a daughter, to be a friend, and on and on. I planted my ambition on a garden of self-hatred. The women who saw my bravado had no idea how I berated and belittled myself if I were not successful every minute of the day. They had no idea that I suffered beneath the pressure I placed on myself to constantly achieve, afraid the foundation around me would break apart and I would be discovered as a fraud. The messages I gave to myself were cruel, filled with words I would never say to another person. They sounded like my mother's voice.

I certainly had my work cut out for me in therapy. I had always embraced hard work, but my therapy was demanding. There were times when delving into my pain manifested in such intestinal spasms, I could not get a bowl of tomato soup into my body. Those usually had to do with the inability to adequately describe how minimal I felt—as if I could, should, disappear, how everyone would be better off without me, even as I knew I could never leave willingly. Recognizing that exercise could help me cope with my emotions and appreciate my body, I awoke each morning and ran as many as six miles—in the rain, snow, and wind—before work. Many times I ran alone, or with male friends. There were not many women running at that hour in those days. The pressure I put on myself to "be healthy" of body and mind was enormous. The payoff was that I started every day with an accomplishment, something that gave me a modicum of self-respect.

My days were a blur, between working, caring for the girls, and attempting to maintain my relationships by socializing on the weekends with Bruce and my friends. He and I had periods of time when we saw even less of each other, times that required an understanding of his schedule that I could not muster. But we always loved each other, and we grew together from teenagers into the people we are today. Perhaps Bruce sometimes expected more of me than I thought I could handle, but his high expectations and confidence in my abilities pushed me to excel. I did become successful in many ways. First and foremost, our daughters being wonderful mothers, crediting me at times with showing them the path. Additionally, I have had a very interesting career—many, in actuality. I recognized that my need to please him was part of what had motivated my success. Our partnership is stronger today than it has ever been, as

Bruce and I both acknowledge and appreciate the choice we make to love and stay committed to each other each day.

Here is a recognition I have never spoken but know to be true: As much as I have loved Allison and Emily all of their lives, more than words can express, I enjoy them today more than when they were young. Why? Because thanks to medication and therapy, I now feel more relaxed with my daughters than I have ever been before. I love our communication as my daughters share their lives with me. I can't help but reflect back on the families of my college friends and what I wanted most in my life, and although it was so elusive to me then, I treasure it now. I love my confidence in my daughters as I watch them navigate the challenges of their adult lives. I love my joy as I watch my daughters grow and grow. Most of all, I feel at peace, having thrown away the constant need to compare myself to my mother, for I know that the women I mothered are remarkable and amazing.

My mother was lonely, miserable, frightening, and pathetic. She pushed my sisters and me away, even as she cried, begged, for us to love her. "Tell me how to be a better mother, please!" she screamed over and over throughout our lives. But how could children know how to mother? My sisters and I certainly never knew. It has taken me a lifetime to learn that I am not, nor was I ever, my mother. My marriage is not my parents' marriage, and my children are not my sisters. The healing I have done has helped me to live my own life, to overcome my trauma, to grow as a person, and to love myself. Having built my own healthy family, I can appreciate my parents, who were, for years, the most important people in shaping my identity. Even while acknowledging their hurtful behaviors, I can accept that my parents loved my sisters and me. This acceptance frees me and makes me whole.

CHAPTER SIXTEEN
A WOMAN OF MANY CAREERS

There were years when I was embarrassed to talk about my professional life. I grew up at a time when women rarely had career aspirations beyond becoming a teacher, nurse, or secretary—all important and respected careers, but none that I desired. Furthermore, when a woman did work outside of the home, she would pursue one career for all or most of her life. With less freedom to explore, women typically stayed in their chosen profession and advanced until they reached their goal or accepted society's limitations. Then they received their "gold watches" and retired. I was not that woman. I had wanderlust, at least when it came to all the careers that beckoned to me. I wanted to try my hand at every one of my interests, and I was fortunate enough to have many opportunities to do so, as well as a financially successful husband to provide for our needs.

My master's degree was in speech and language pathology, and I earned it at night while working as a public school speech therapist during the day. My interest lay in a particular aspect of therapy focused on the swallowing musculature and how it impacted the dentition being corrected with orthodontia, and I built a practice helping orthodontic or future orthodontic patients whose ways of swallowing had affected the arrangement of their teeth. Many of my patients needed to retrain their tongues in order to improve their dentition.

However, eventually, my lifelong interest in fashion called to me like the sirens, and I faced a fork in the road. I had lost my zeal for therapy after years of working with many patients and had a practice to sell to a younger speech therapist. I decided to do so and gamble on my ability to be noticed in the fashion arena. Macy's was hiring stylists to upsell on the Ready to Wear selling floor, and I applied and was offered a position at the closest location to my home. I had no idea how the system worked but knew I had a well-trained eye not only for how garments should be worn but by whom, particularly as more women were entering the corporate world and needed wardrobing. Fortunately, I became noticed enough on the sales floor to bring the human resources manager of training to meet me. I was thrilled to be offered the role of Ready to Wear fashion trainer for Macy's Northeast. Now in my mid-thirties, I finally had my dream job.

It was my first time working for a corporation. Even though I knew that few could rival my ability to dress a woman, I had little experience with the politics of the workplace. It was also a time when women, who had to fight their way to the top, were still pushed down, often by other women. Excelling as the fashion trainer helped me catch the eye of a woman I admired, who then recruited me to work in her department. She had a terrible reputation for being unkind, even abusive. But I was used to that combination, so I was up for the job—or so I thought. At the same time, Emily was struggling with learning issues related to her anatomy. Soon I faced the dilemma so many women before and after me have faced: my child or my career. Had my manager been one with whom I could discuss my challenges, I may have been able to stay at Macy's in some capacity, but that was not the case. I left and became a freelancer for them, moderating fashion seminars and dressing models for fashion shows for years.

Thus my freelance business was born, and I loved that role as well. Fashion shows, personal shopping, makeup artistry, accessorizing—I did it all—and built a thriving business called Style Unlimited. My confidence in my creativity soared, and that led to a position with Wakefern/ShopRite Supermarkets, where I organized themed festivals and special events at stores. My manager and I would create the themes and invite vendors to provide food samples for customers. These one-to-two-day events proved popular, and I became responsible for the success of each event, from top to bottom. Often staying in motels for days at a time, I continued to run my miles, regardless of where I was or what time I had to make it to the store to set up.

And then, I had my first small bowel obstruction, which perforated my bowels and nearly ended my life. That fight began my decades-long battle with obstructions caused by adhesions, the slow motility with which I had always fought, and concomitant issues. That battle lasted from 1993 to 2014, when I underwent my twenty-third abdominal surgery, my ileostomy.

During those years, I continued to explore so many of my interests and translate them into careers. I worked as a makeup artist, personal shopper, and closet organizer. I even dressed and then packed suitcases for busy career women. My business partner, dear friend Carol, and I moved seniors into assisted living facilities and did interior design to enhance their adjustment into their new lives. Together, we were a team of hardworking seniors ourselves, understanding what was relevant and important as our clients downsized. I found my voice as a writer, penning articles from *The Phoenix*, a magazine for life as an ostomate, to *The Connection*, a commerce magazine that circulates through several areas in New Jersey, publishing my first book, maintaining a daily, and then weekly, blog for years. My daily blog was entitled *Wardrobe Wizard,* and my second was *More Than My Ostomy*. I even assisted with skin care and aesthetic consulting for a facial plastic surgeon. I am so proud to be publishing this, my second book. While I cannot draw a line, straight or wavy, my creative side constantly longs to express itself visually, and so I express myself each day as I dress. I am often teased because rather than following the casual style women in our area prefer, I dress up to go to the supermarket. But I am my own Barbie doll, and I value every opportunity to "play dress-up." My inner child is satisfied; her artistic expression is liberated.

While I am grateful for the financial compensation I have received from my many jobs over the years, my most rewarding is my volunteer work mentoring fellow ostomates and facilitating our support-group meetings. Nothing could ever rival the satisfaction I feel in helping uplift others in my community. This work provides me with invaluable rewards. The funny thing is when we are in our seventies, nobody expects us to work, but I love to be able to continue making a difference.

Recently, I was visiting a new doctor who asked, "Are you employed or retired?" I stated, "I am retired. However, I am a writer, an advocate, a mentor, a motivational speaker, a support-group facilitator." I meet ostomates where they are in their acceptance and ability to embrace their new anatomy with gratitude for their lifesaving surgery. The gift I can give them is my knowledge they will find their way because I will do all I can to make that happen. These activities define me as much as the total sum of all of my previous positions and fill me with pride. It is amazing to be able to share my story with people who can relate and to see the smiles on their faces when they feel good about their bodies and themselves. This work nourishes my soul more deeply than all of my careers combined. For that opportunity, I am so grateful.

CHAPTER SEVENTEEN
MAJOR SURGERY, MAJOR CHANGES

For quite a while, during each visit to my gynecologist, I heard the same recommendation: a hysterectomy. At age forty-three, I finally acquiesced. Large fibroid tumors had grown into my cervix, making sex increasingly painful, and my insides felt so bulky in my small frame that when I stood up, it felt as though they needed time to follow.

"Have it done!" my doctor promised. "You will be the healthiest you have ever been, and it will help your anatomy to remove your swollen uterus since it puts pressure on your bowels!" What a carrot for a lifetime of intestinal dysfunction.

Almost immediately after my hysterectomy, I felt reborn. My bowels responded to minimal combinations of fiber and laxatives, and I went back to running the six miles a day I had run for years. Gratitude guided my every step. I envisioned a bright future as Allison was excited to begin her freshman year at Lehigh University, and I looked forward to spending time with Emily, who was still in high school. There was a peace behind my eyes, a vision of a proud mother, a sexy wife, a productive and loving family woman.

During these months, my mother and I finally had a détente. She divorced my stepfather, Bob, and although she missed him terribly, she knew it was the right thing to do. My sisters and I had encouraged her to leave him since she was so unhappy in her life with him. They had been married for close to two decades, and he had assuaged her loneliness after my father's death. My mother had met Bob at a dance on a Saturday night, about eighteen months after my father died, and hadn't known him more than two weeks before becoming engaged to him. She introduced us to Bob the following Saturday, a week before they married. My sisters and I were in shock, and angry. Who was Bob? We knew nothing about him, but we knew that our mother was marrying him impulsively. My sisters and I stood under the chuppah and cried. Our young father, only forty-five years old, was gone, and now we were supposed to be celebrating the new man in her life, this stranger, moving into our home, their bed?

But acceptance is wondrous. Time passes, and even the worst reality becomes acceptable. After marrying him, my mother raged at Bob, rather than at my sisters and me most of the time. So in that way, he insulated us from her. Our transgressions suddenly meant less because his were so much worse. Their volatility became our peace. The seesaw who was my mother felt satisfied with her anger at him, and so we received less of it for the first time.

And then she was alone, their marriage dissolved after eighteen years, as if it had never been. *Poof*, it was here, and *poof*, it was gone. My mother and Bob ended in the same way they had tempestuously begun. They had spoken of divorce shortly into their marriage and, finally, eighteen years later, decided to live apart. He left her, sick with metastatic breast cancer, to clean out and divest herself of the home in which they had lived.

Three months after my hysterectomy, my life transformed, once again. Our family was at a belated Chanukah celebration at Michele and Ira's house when a pain crushed me onto the floor. I actually thought I had been shot or knifed and looked around for the perpetrator. The true cause was a catastrophic bowel obstruction. A spaghetti-like strand of scar tissue had perforated my small intestines. Bruce was able to get me into the car, my projectile vomiting unstoppable, and take me home, where we called the doctor. But it was a Sunday night, and we received no return phone call. Bruce had to leave me to go to the train, half an hour away, to pick up

Allison, who was returning from a visit to a friend. It was snowing quite hard. Traveling was slow and difficult, and Bruce had instructed Emily to stay by me and call the emergency squad if she felt it necessary. We were so unsophisticated, never having been in that type of situation. As my vomiting continued and I lay on the floor in our primary bathroom, I whispered to Emily she should call the police. I knew I was losing ground. The squad arrived, and by now, the agony was worse, coming in waves, similar but so much worse than transition labor. I began to beg anyone in ear range to shoot me, each wave of peristalsis strangling my bowel tighter and tighter. Due to the snow in our particularly hilly area, I was brought to the local emergency room. Poor Emily was left home to wait for Bruce to return and pick her up to meet me at the hospital. She was terrified. I was x-rayed and told since I was at a party at my sister's house, I had gastroenteritis, and they gave me fluids and codeine to calm the spasms. This misdiagnosis almost ended my life.

I was so sick. Calling out from Wakefern the next day, I could barely speak. I was weak, which we assumed was from all of the vomiting. Bruce left for his office, putting Allison in charge of watching over me. We still believed I had gastroenteritis, and since my symptoms changed, it seemed to make sense. That change actually occurred because, unbeknownst to us, my bowel had perforated, and since now all of the poisonous matter in my intestines were released into my abdomen, like a pipe under the sink that bursts, the pressure released and I felt no pain. We assumed the worst had passed. On the contrary, I was rotting internally. Over the next several hours, Bruce kept watch but didn't understand the mechanism at work in my body. By Tuesday, my skin looked green and I lay in bed unable to take a sip of water. I told Bruce I had to call in sick again, and they would probably fire me, but Bruce called on my behalf. By late morning, Bruce told me to call my internist, unaware I was deathly ill. Looking back, our naivete almost cost me my life. I could barely speak with the receptionist, who gave me an appointment later in the day but obviously sensed I was in extremis. Dr. Lipschutz called me within a few minutes and, hearing my inability to speak, had me come right over. Taking one look at my bright-red distended abdomen, he ordered blood stat and told me I was acutely ill. I kept asking if I had cancer, and all he could say was that I was acutely ill. He supported me as I stumbled to the car, fearing an ambulance would take too long, and told Allison to drive me to a different medical center than Sunday night, immediately. What we learned is that once I perforated, my abdomen had filled with material that was toxic and deadly, which was affecting all of my organs, and I was only hours from death. I underwent surgery to remove close to three feet of ileum, the lowest section of the small intestine. Following this surgery came peritonitis, pancreatitis, irreparable damage to my gallbladder, and temporary damage to my kidneys. After months in the hospital, I was hoping to resume my life.

When the colorectal surgeon told me I might need an ostomy, my mother screamed, "No!" She feared I would be "disfigured" and, frankly, "disgusting." At that time, we knew little about the lifesaving procedure. I did not have an ostomy, and I fought back from the brink of death through sheer willpower. The loving support from my wonderful family gave me determination to live. Three months later, just as I was getting back on my feet, another adhesion strangled my mid-jejunum, causing the loss of another two and a half feet of small intestine. My colorectal surgeon, Dr. Groff, and the infectious disease physician, Dr. Greenman, saved me once again.

Throughout the next twenty-one years, adhesions (scar tissue), bowel obstructions, slow motility, emergency rooms, and operating rooms became my life. Bruce and I lived from hospital visit to hospital visit, and thankfully, Dr. Starker, my surgeon for many of my surgeries, was the head of my team. Sadly, however, my vision of visiting Allison at Lehigh University, walking with her with pride across the same campus Bruce had attended, my hopes of spending even more time with Emily, laughing as we usually did, and all the other wondrous plans I had for travel and good times ahead disappeared.

My gastroenterologist, Dr. Lerer, and colorectal surgeon sent me to all of the revered meccas known for treating unique situations. At the Mayo Clinic in Rochester, Minnesota, I had a subtotal colectomy in May 2001. This intervention proved successful for five years, until my rectum stopped functioning. That new challenge led to years of small bowel blockages, lysis (removal) of adhesions, even more blockages, and ultimately, a life I could not fully live. My potentially life-threatening episodes, with sudden onsets that could strike at any time, made Bruce and me feel so uncertain about the future that we stopped making plans. But I walked four miles daily, worked at my various careers, saw the family when I could, and was intimate with Bruce. Together, we made the best of living with a sword hanging over us.

Eventually, during my twenty-third abdominal surgery, and after twenty-one years of suffering, I was finally offered an ileostomy, a procedure which diverts stool from the small intestines to a pouch that covers a stoma. Not only did this experience save my life, it gave me a new purpose. I am a national advocate for the United Ostomy Associations of America (UOAA), and one of a handful of members of its patient advisory board. In 2019, having shepherded to completion the outpatient Ostomy Center of Overlook Hospital in Summit, New Jersey, I was honored by the UOAA as Mighty Advocate of the Year. The center allows patients to receive care from wound and ostomy continence nurses after leaving the security of the hospital.

I have always desired to use my voice to advocate for others. I am happy that I have been able to bring the oral presentation and training skills I learned in my career to my roles in the ostomy community. Contributing to the patient advisory board also offers me an opportunity to examine the many issues—social, physical, financial, and political—facing ostomates across the country, and sometimes weigh in on legislation that can create a positive impact on the ostomy community. I have written a book entitled *So Much More Than My Ostomy: Loving My Perfectly Imperfect Body!* I have mentored hundreds of ostomates in accepting and adjusting to their new anatomy. I have launched three ostomy support groups in New Jersey, and I lead a thriving monthly ostomy support group online, a group filled with amazing people living their best lives.

I even coordinated a fashion show at the 2019 UOAA national conference. The final event of the conference, our fashion show ended with a standing ovation! Bruce and my daughters and sons-in-law were there to support me as I served as commentator for the fashion show. Hearing my family and community applaud for my fellow ostomates, some having two stomas, I realized how very fortunate I was, how lucky to have the ability to help a dozen women, some with their pouches not just visible but decorated, feel like the stars they were as they sashayed down the runway and took their bows.

I want you to know that I was not blessed with immediate acceptance of my new body. On March 17, 2014, I had my procedure. I healed so quickly and was so determined to begin my new life that I left the hospital after three days. Bruce brought me home, and as was "our usual dance" after I returned from the hospital, I went straight into the shower. Of course, in the hospital, I had not seen my new anatomy. Pleased with my stoma medically, my surgeon had cheerfully sent me on my way, with a follow-up appointment in two weeks. Now, leaving the shower, I grabbed my towel, wrapped it around myself, and walked to the mirror. When I saw the bag hanging from my abdomen, I began to scream. *What had I done to myself?* How could I face myself again? How would Bruce ever want to hold me, be intimate with me?

Bruce came running into the bathroom and found me on the floor sobbing. I sobbed for the years of hell we had endured; I sobbed for all I had missed in the lives of our daughters; I sobbed because I was an emaciated woman with a terribly scarred abdomen, which now had a pouch hanging from it. I cried for everything I had overcome in my life, and I cried because I was afraid I would not be able to survive this latest blow. Bruce held me in his arms and told me he was in awe of me, in awe of my strength and bravery, of my determination to survive and to succeed. That was the one and only time I cried about my ostomy. From that point on, I was on a mission to help others feel pride and power and appreciation and gratitude for this lifesaving surgery, as I truly do today.

In January 1993, while I was at my sickest, fighting for my life through peritonitis and sepsis, my mother became my hero! She came to the hospital every day for months. She helped me wash, as she had when I was a child. She brought my favorite nibbles to spark my lack of appetite. As she held my hand, we shared a love I had never known existed between us. Even when I heard her telling people how sick I was, somehow I felt that her presence was protecting me. Having stayed up the entire night watching the vancomycin drip into my intravenous lines, I still relaxed each morning when she arrived.

This antibiotic, so caustic it would blow my IV lines, was supposed to be lifesaving. But how was it supposed to save my life when it was only infiltrating my veins and not traveling quickly enough into my bloodstream? One of my doctors told me that he would find a line in my feet if necessary, but that was cold comfort. This was before the usage in our medical center of the PICC line, a central catheter threaded through the upper arm/shoulder region into the superior vena cava in the chest. So each time I was infused with the antibiotic, a new line needed to be created in my arm. My nights were filled with worry that my narrow arms would not offer another place for a line and that my feet were next. Fortunately, I was one of the first to take advantage of the revolutionary PICC line. My doctors informed me they felt they were going to lose me otherwise. The PICC line proved to be a lifesaver, mine at the time.

Throughout those months when I could not advocate for myself, my mother advocated for me. She reminded the nurses of my needs. She informed them that I needed clean nightgowns and my bed changed. She alerted them when my line was clogged, when the machinery that tracked my tubes was beeping. With her big beautiful smile, she was irresistible.

She even fluffed my pillows and smoothed my sheets every time I was able to get out of bed.

Three months later, in April 1993, when I required another major surgery and lengthy hospitalization, my mother came to visit me again. This time, I noticed that she had experienced a marked decline in her health. She couldn't walk the halls and required the staff to bring her by wheelchair to my room. She was thin, pale, and less coherent. Yet I was so preoccupied with my own health that I didn't pay much attention to the changes in her. She explained that she needed oxygen for COPD, a result of tuberculosis as a child, and that answer satisfied me at the time. I had lost track of what was happening in her life, fighting for mine. Sadly, her breast cancer, of which neither of us was yet aware, had metastasized, spreading to her lungs, and she was already losing her ability to breathe.

While I was recuperating at home, I recognized that my mother now needed me as never before. My sisters were working. Michele and Ira owned a shop called Michele's Kitchen's Take Along Gourmet, and Mindy was a school psychologist. I was on medical leave. So I took on more of the caregiving for our mother and accompanied her to medical appointments.

At one such appointment, her doctor found a walnut-sized lesion on her breastbone and told me to feel it. It was as hard as a rock. "Mom!" I cried. "How long have you had this?" Her voice retreated then and there, never—at least in my memory—to speak sense again. She replied in sounds reminiscent of the gibberish prayers she had uttered while atoning for eating too much each Shabbat. From that moment on, only she would understand the words she spoke.

Later, after her death, as my sisters and I cleaned out her nightstand, we found multiple letters from a radiologist clearly informing my mother of a suspicious lesion found on her mammogram that required further imaging. While my mother had lived in fear of cancer all her life, she had, ironically, ignored these messages from the radiologist, just as she had ignored the many follow-up messages from our gynecologist. Unfortunately, due to HIPAA law privacy regulations, our gynecologist, the same surgeon who had performed my hysterectomy, had not been able to reveal to me that my mother needed to see a surgeon.

My sisters and I, good girls as we had always been, now became sentinels over our mother's health. We brought our mother to a surgeon who removed the malignant lump. Based on his initial findings, he believed that, with treatment, she could survive the cancer. Whether he was unaware of the extent of the metastasis or merely wanted to provide hope for us, he did not tell us the truth. Her breathing was so compromised that she needed more oxygen, and she was, more and more, retreating into her own world.

My mother had lost her fight and her spirit. By the end of her life, just two or three months later, she was unable to communicate, having returned to what my sisters and I considered her own comfortable world. We could no longer understand the language she spoke. We wondered if this was the voice of cancer metastasized to her brain, or mental illness. In the end, the cause of her death was recurring double pneumonia, a result of lung cancer.

When my mother died, my sisters and I, once again, stood on one another's shoulders and held one another as each of us needed. Our mother had been such a source of pain and sadness, but we loved her, we absolutely loved her. At my father's funeral, she separated herself from us. Yet at her funeral, my sisters and I clung to her casket and spoke loving words. In our eulogy for her, we were not false. We acknowledged that she had been an unhappy woman her entire life, but we still found enough to share that was loving: her smile, her ability to charm people, her glamorous beauty. She would have been proud of us.

I will always remember how my mother gave me all the love she had at the time in my life when I needed her more than I ever had before. As brief as those months in the hospital were in comparison to the years of abuse I had endured in her home, it felt glorious to have my mother beside me, plumping my pillows, straightening my sheets, bringing me corn muffins. She gave me courage, she gave me confidence, she gave me her smile. I tried to do the same for her as she faced her greatest challenge, but she had already escaped into a world I could not reach.

Writing *The Best We Could* has given me the opportunity to openly share the true story of my love for my mother with all of its heartbreaking moments. I used to ask each therapist what they thought my life would have been like had I been raised with safety and stability, had I not had to spend my childhood simply surviving. Each of them, in their own words, pointed out that I would not be the same, and perhaps, as I have come to agree over the years, I would not be as strong. Which other abilities do I believe I would not have acquired? The thought that most resonates with me is this: Most likely, I would not know, truly know, that even if you do not feel loved, that doesn't mean you are not. There is power in that realization.

CHAPTER EIGHTEEN
REBIRTH

I am grateful that I have finished this memoir, which I started and stopped countless times, perhaps over decades. Once I knew my parents were different, I couldn't stop knowing it. Finally sharing my story, emerging from shame and the pressure to hide, feels like rebirth.

I no longer feel unlovable or unloved by my parents. I choose to believe that, in their way, they loved my sisters and me and did the best they could. My parents had other choices they could have made. They could have chosen to seek support or treatment for their mental illnesses. They could have chosen to learn better ways to parent my sisters and me. Yet they also could have sent my sisters and me away, or even walked away from us. Still, they chose to raise us to the best of their ability, at the same time struggling with their own traumas. How exhausting that struggle must have been for them; I know it was for us.

It is no longer necessary for me to waste countless minutes of my life wishing for a different childhood, one of being nurtured, guided, and caressed by innocence. To do so would mean that my life has been unfulfilling, and nothing could be further from the truth! I count my blessings, sometimes several times a day. I recognize with an enormous amount of gratitude the dynamic life Bruce and I have created, the loving marriage and true partnership we have built; Allison and Emily, who are stable, productive, and caring women, wives, and mothers; their adoring husbands, Dave and Jeremy, good men I am fortunate enough to love; and the multi-talented children my daughters and their husbands have raised, Jake, Jessie, Maddie, and Max, who are the joys of my grandparenthood; the love I have for my two sisters, Michele and Mindy; my brother-in-law Ira who has been a brother for most of my life; Bruce's sister Mindy, another sister (how many get to love two Mindys?); my mother-in-law, Eleanor, who was like a mother to me; our entire family; my many friends; the world of ostomates I have met, and those I will meet in the years ahead.

On my road of recovery and acceptance, I have engaged several therapists who met me where I was. Each one gave me new perspectives, insights I would not have been able to absorb until that time. I have always believed that when the student is ready, the teacher will come, and not a minute before or after. Yet no matter how much I grew from my therapists' guidance, the hole in my soul remained. I still felt unloved by the first people in my world, my parents.

Throughout my life, that wound manifested itself in my desire to be loved by everyone I met. From my toddler years onward, my people-pleasing never ceased. Disappointing or upsetting anyone, including people I barely knew, felt as though it threatened my body and soul. I was so afraid to ask for anything, since my mother only took from all of us, that I always needed to be the one doing the giving. I thought that was helping others, but I now see my over-giving often made others think I did not believe them capable of doing for themselves or giving anything to me. These bad habits have taken me a great deal of work to undo. But the effort, like so many others, has been well worth it. Being an equal is a wonderful accomplishment, and I no longer have to be the one to overdo in order to be liked.

Over the years, my relationship with Bruce was the one that suffered most from the impact of my people-pleasing. I wanted him to believe he had made the right choice in marrying me, so I let him guide me, carrying me around in his pocket. I falsely believed that if I could please him, if I did everything right, then he would always love me. I was behaving like a child, not like a wife. I needed him to show me and to tell me how to act, and he fell right into that role, since I believed I needed to be molded. In the early years of our marriage, I saw myself as amorphous, without a true form, having no place anywhere, and needing to fit myself into others' needs. Our Saturday night dates with friends often ended with my asking Bruce, "Was I okay tonight? Did I say or do anything wrong?" But the more I pandered to Bruce and to others, the worse I felt about myself, and perhaps the worse Bruce felt as well. My mother had seen my father as her ticket out of her family life, and ironically, perhaps I had seen Bruce in that same way.

For Bruce and me to build the relationship I wanted, a marriage based on equality and interdependence, I had to work hard in my therapy, shift my perspectives, and make changes in my life. I learned that I had a stable, optimistic, and loving personality. I chose to see the good in us as a couple, and to be the good in life. That desire to see and be good could help me become Bruce's wife and matriarch of the family I wanted to create with him. Yet I had to recognize that this desire wasn't enough. I had to develop a voice and use it. I had to learn how to say when I was not pleased or I disagreed.

Learning how to assert my reality, even when that meant challenging Bruce's, was so difficult for me—and for him too, I am certain. I had to risk him getting angry at me, perhaps acting in a way that he had never seen before, a way he could not predict. But of course, I had never seen him react to my challenging his authority. I always did everything he wanted me to do. I had never openly made the waves that I felt internally. Ultimately, I knew that in order for Bruce and me to grow stronger together, I would have to grow stronger myself. This was the real risk I had to determine was worth taking.

At last, I recognized Bruce would still love me even when I disappointed or disagreed with him, even when I made those waves he might not like. He did not go to sleep, pull away, slam doors, or threaten me. He may not have liked how I expressed myself, but he stayed with me and listened as we worked through my feelings. We talked honestly about the reality that if I couldn't be myself, grow to accept myself, and become my best self, I would lose myself. There were no alternatives. Additionally, I pointed out to him that he deserved a wife who was happy, who would create the happy family he too wanted. He was smart enough and, I suppose, loved me enough to support my growth. And I am happy to say that I believe the effort has been worthwhile for both of us .... We have everything we have wanted in each other.

I knew that in order to become my authentic self, I would need to learn to see myself as enough. That word might sound simple, but for a woman who had never felt that way, accepting it was a huge challenge. The effort was draining, albeit extremely valuable. I took baby steps toward self-confidence, stretching myself toward new, but achievable, goals. My running, for example, began with a few steps in the backyard. These led me to road races and more and more miles. I was amazed at my determination, at how trustworthy my body was, and at how great I felt to accomplish a goal each morning.

From there, I had to work on taking action because I wanted to, not because it would make someone else think better of me or say nice things about me. I began to pursue activities that allowed me to serve my community, again, not because I needed accolades, but because I felt good doing good. The more I gave back to others, the better I felt. I began to teach aerobics to help motivate other women of my age to feel stronger and more fit. When the fitness club where I worked told me I was too old for the young crowd they hoped to attract (and I was all of thirty-five years old), the women in my class signed a petition asking for me to continue as their instructor. It didn't change my plans to move on. I knew I was never going to be happy working for an ageist company. But I was quite happy to know I had made a difference in the lives of these women my own age, enough of a difference that they wanted me to stay.

Simultaneously, I reset my "Saturday night rules" and told Bruce he was off duty, that I was confident I would be fine without an end-of-the-night critique. My decision freed both of us to simply enjoy ourselves. I had wasted so much of my life worrying about the potential negative effects of my words and actions on others, always replaying the evening, judging myself and feeling a failure. If there is one thing I have taught my daughters throughout their lives, it is to not worry about what others think of you. "Just do your best and enjoy your lives!" What a sense of freedom that signals to them. And yet, I held myself to such an unattainable standard of pleasing everyone. An unwinnable game I played. How sad. I am so grateful to report that my daughters have given the same advice not only to their daughters but also back to me. Allison and Emily are comfortable sharing their viewpoints with me because they know they are kind and caring women. I admire, and aspire to, the way they support others while remaining true to their own points of view.

As I forged my own identity, I also put enormous effort into differentiating my behavior from my parents' unreliability. At first, if I could not be at school to pick up my daughters on time, I would become hysterical, terrified they would feel abandoned. How unhealthy for all of us. If, while we were shopping, Allison or Emily wandered off to say hello to a friend, I would crumble, so enormous was my fear that my child was lost to me forever. I agonized constantly. But my growing recognition that I was not my mother proved eye opening, if also a bit scary. If I were not my mother, then who was I? My journey of self-discovery would have to continue.

In my conversations with Allison and Emily as adults, they have shared that they never once feared I would abandon them, nor did they ever feel I did not love or treasure them. They knew I was a responsible parent, perhaps overly responsible. My hand went up the minute a volunteer was needed for anything and everything in which they were involved. I ran fashion shows for their PTA for years, drove other children to events so they were with friends, and more. They never had a reason to question whether they could trust me. If I said I would do something, I would do it. My daughters reflected that I always made them my priority on the weekends, finding things they would enjoy. They remembered the three of us sharing car rides, shopping trips, and lunches out. They recalled that I had always treated them, along with Bruce, as the most important people in my life, which they were.

I do regret one mistake I made as a parent, however. At times, when I was filled with grief, remembering the abuse I had suffered when I was the same age as one of the girls, I would tell her about my traumatic experiences. My daughters were not meant to absorb my grief, and my confiding in my children as if they were adults placed upon them a burden they did not need to bear. In a way, my actions remind me of my mother seizing every opportunity she had to tell my sisters and me how terrible her life was. I had tried to heal my mother, and perhaps I had wanted my daughters to heal me, but I quickly regretted it.

So here I am at this moment in my life, looking back on this Herculean effort to tell my story. Had I not been engaged in demanding, but important, work with Susan Trutt, PhD, who refused to believe, or allow me to believe, that I was not wanted or loved by my parents, I would have written this book in a very different way. The time was right to write. Once again, the student was ready, and the teacher came.

Susan helped me to separate my parents' love from their struggles to express it. As I have come to understand that my parents were trapped in cycles of trauma, my father's bipolar disorder and my mother's borderline personality disorder no longer define them in my heart, and I no longer define myself as someone whose parents didn't love her.

Three times my mother tried to end her pregnancies by throwing herself down flights of stairs. "You see?" I shouted to Susan. "That is proof she didn't want any of us!" But Susan stood her ground. "That was before she knew you. Once she knew you, she wanted to love you."

I still have work to do, but the progress I am making is energizing. Here in my seventies, a time that leads many of us toward acceptance, I am still striving to emerge more fully formed. I know my life is entering a new chapter filled with hope. I am a complete woman, grateful for all I have learned, who I have become, and what more I will achieve.

Recently, I have made progress in recognizing the positive qualities of my parents and in seeing how I both carry on and reshape their legacy clearly. My mother had a radiant smile and a high social intelligence. I believe that was her gift, her superpower. People were attracted to her and wanted to be in her sphere. She showed my sisters and me how to be a people person in the best ways possible, how to show interest in others, how to care for and about others. Today my sisters and I are all helpers, always the first to reach out when we believe someone may need help. Unlike my mother, however, we are not looking for praise or indebtedness in return. We are simply happy to do what we can.

My father had a wonderful sense of humor and a twinkle in his eyes. He was smart as a whip, brilliant in math, musical, and charismatic. I adore all of these beautiful characteristics, see them in different ways in his grandchildren and my grandchildren. I believe my sisters and I carry on these characteristics as well. Most of all, I deeply appreciate these qualities when I see them reflected in others. They are as a magnet to me, pulling me closer.

So now you have seen my parents, and you have seen me, a woman who has lived a very full and successful life. I have been a daughter, a sister, a wife, a mother, a friend, a grandparent, a speech therapist, a fashion trainer for a major department store chain, a special events coordinator, a makeup artist, a skin care and beauty consultant, a motivational speaker, a fashion show coordinator and commentator, an interior designer for senior citizens, a patient advocate, a support-group facilitator, a mentor, and a writer. Everything I have done in my life, I now recognize, has allowed me to bring beauty into others' worlds or uplift others' voices. I have received so much joy from seeing others smiling back at me. In fact, helping others express themselves helped inspire me to finally tell my own story.

I can speak to sadness, loss, grief, and emptiness, but I can also speak to survival, growth, beauty, and happiness. I still have work to do. Like anyone who suffered trauma, I am still healing and probably will be for the rest of my life. But I do it now with a fully formed adult brain. Rather than resent that I wasted much of my earlier years fighting so many battles for survival, I am now recognizing that the life I have is because of the battles I have fought. I look ahead, with excitement, to each and every day, each and every opportunity to continue to grow from all I experience along the way.

ACKNOWLEDGMENTS

Thank you for reading *The Best We Could: Healing from Intergenerational Trauma*. As I have mentioned, it is an empowering feeling to complete this memoir as part of the healing that has taken place throughout my life. Intergenerational trauma is pervasive, so perhaps it will resonate with many who have healed or are still healing.

Sharing my story now is timely because my parents are gone, and my daughters remind me they are no longer young mothers—three of my four grandchildren are college age, and our youngest grandchild is already driving. My sisters and I are recognizing the signs of aging we cannot deny. It is safe to say there is no time like the present to bring awareness of "the family who lived next door," whose experiences were, most probably, so different from other neighbors.

Thinking of myself as the "Keeper of the Stories" is a responsibility I take very seriously. Everything, other than the hearsay of my grandparents' stories and the way my parents actually met, gleaned from those who knew their history, I have written from my own experiences and firsthand knowledge.

I have spent so much of my life feeling "less than" or "not enough" that I am joyful for my self-acceptance today. I have worked hard to arrive here rather than accept my own negative feelings about myself. I could have wallowed in self-destruction. I know that to be true. But never would I have opened the door to this moment of peace were it not for many in my life. I acknowledge them with love, adoration, gratitude, and undying devotion.

Thank you, first, to my parents, Lillian and Herman (Hy) Finkel, for doing the best they could. Without their desire, love, and determination, as difficult as it was for them to keep us together, our lives would have been extremely different.

Michele Zaitz and Mindy Smith, my everlasting two-thirds of a complex puzzle, this one heart we share is as rare as a perfect triangle. Without their sides, I would have been unable to stand. They are my Forever Gifts. I thank them for supporting me, leaving their own lives to help me with my health issues, never needing to be asked, simply saying, "I will be there!" Many times, every time, I could count on them. Regardless of where I was in seeking or obtaining better health, they were with me, holding my hand.

If we are fortunate, we have that one teacher who finds in us something special, something worth cultivating. My sixth-grade teacher, Edna S. Brady, for that is how she signed everything, was just that person. I came into her class with the lowest self-esteem in my life, and she saw that "something special" in me, or simply made me feel it existed. I truly believe she was the first to do so. She gave me extra projects, helped me find my creativity, and never missed an opportunity to say something encouraging, even when I came to school with a tear-stained face. At the end of the year, she wrote in my autograph book, "May time never wither, nor custom never change, your infinite variety." I never forgot how she made me feel .... I had infinite variety, even as I didn't know that to be true until all these years later. I am filled with gratitude that she wrote something she must have written hundreds of times, to hundreds of students. But this one student felt value for the first time in her life!

When Bruce Mantell and I married, we spoke the usual vows, "For better or for worse, in sickness and in health." He has proven to be my love partner each and every day, in each and every way. Days and nights in the emergency room, waiting outside the operating room, putting his shoulder near mine while I cried a million tears, fought a million battles, if only in my nightmares. He is mine in ways unimaginable, and I am his. Finding each other as teens meant growing together, not an easy feat for either of us. However, as seventy-somethings, we can look back on a lifetime of challenges and trials, as all couples do, I believe. But we have the wonderful opportunity to grow from looking back, as well as ahead, to shared hopes and dreams. A deep love and appreciation, what greater accomplishment for each of us, for both of us?

There are still times, fifty years later, when I look at our daughters, Allison Gollin and Emily Golden, and pinch myself. Am I the same woman who gave birth to them? How did they grow to be these magnificent women? They are wives, moms with careers, daughters and daughters-in-law, sisters and sisters-in-law, nieces, friends, outstanding and giving members of society. They have aspirations and goals, which I have no doubt they will fulfill, and I see the joy they give and receive, the stability they are for so many.

The next generation, our four grandchildren, Jake and Jessie Gollin (the JJs) and Maddie and Max Golden (the M&Ms), are the secret sauce of life! They make everything better, more delicious. Watching them grow and navigate their world is a gift their parents presented us. And I love their fathers, Dave Gollin and Jeremy Golden, as our own children. There could be no other way. It is amazing how we were able to have our hearts grow bigger as we welcomed these wonderful men into our family.

My sister-in-law, Mindy Mantell-Kardan, and my brother-in-law, Ira Zaitz, are as dear to me as my blood relatives and have been threads in the fabric of my life for over sixty years. How do I define such relationships? We have all shown our devotion countless times and know we can count on each other, always. I love them with all my heart, and I treasure growing with them.

My darling in-laws, Eleanor and Murray Mantell, are gifts I received when I married their son, but more than that, they stepped in when we became a family. They included my mother and my sisters and their families at every holiday table; they were "my" parents as much as they were Bruce and Mindy's. They never wavered in their love and devotion. When I had major surgery at the Mayo Clinic in Rochester, Minnesota, they flew there to help me recover, staying in a hotel for two weeks, walking with me a few steps at a time, until I recovered my energy. These are blessings I treasure with overwhelming gratitude. They showed me I was as important to them as their own children.

Dorothy Montecalvo was the substitute mama Alli and Emily needed when I was a working mother. She sat with them during their homework, transported them to activities, bathed and fed them, and loved them dearly. They loved her dearly as well. The day this beautiful woman answered my ad for a sitter was the day my heart reached to hers, and I knew she would fill the piece I was unable to provide, and she never, never let us down. Her devotion to our family was beautiful, and she taught me so much about being a mother.

My friends, of which I am so fortunate to have countless, are the golden filaments in the tapestry of art in my life. We share so much, and like the many flavors of ice cream I enjoy, each of you adds a special ingredient, and I am so fortunate to love all of you and the enrichment you provide. I can't name all of you and will undoubtedly forget someone, so I will just say that you mean so much to me and have taught me more than you know. The love I feel for each of you is like a petal on the most gorgeous flower, filling me with joy.

Lisa Kaplan Gordon deserves special recognition, not only as a dear friend but as my initial editor. Her inquisitive nature pushed me to go deeper to respond to her myriad questions. I imagine from the time she was a small child, she asked *Why?* over and over again. Thank you, Lisa, for affirming my story needed to be told, and although there were no answers to some of the whys, you acknowledged that was part of the reason to write my memoir. It is okay to not always have explanations or find solutions, and it is okay to admit sometimes that it is better to simply accept that what you see is really what is in front of you.

Thanks to all of my therapists over the years who met me where I was in my growth and acceptance. And a most special statement of gratitude to Susan Trutt, PhD. She came into my life at a time when I believed that, although I could feel loved by so many, I could not feel loved by my parents. Susan turned my head and heart in a totally different direction, and I am eternally grateful. Among the many gifts she has given me with her knowledge and time, the work we did regardless of how difficult for each of us, was her admonishment when I would respond with my usual, "I know they didn't love me. I wasn't worthy and I am flawed." She would have none of it, and as we worked together and I matured in my thinking, I realized that story was just that, a story I told myself. She reminded me each week how much my parents sacrificed to love and keep all of us together. She put the last piece of the puzzle on the board, helping me to see there is celebration in seeing it all come together, regardless of how dark it appeared at times.

My writing sisters at Broken Sound Club, all marvelous women, so accomplished, led by gifted Sonia Ravech, have supported my writing for many years. We have grown together, and that has helped me dig deeper in my ability to trust the written word to explain what I want to say. I want to thank Ellen Brazer, Blanche Haber, Harriet Lasky, Diane Melton, Pat Rohner, Merle Setren, and Marilyn York for helping me dry my eyes, laugh, and speak my truth, and I hope I have done the same for them.

Amy Klein, you are a wonder! Not only did you help me reframe what my memoir could accomplish, you helped me reach it with your gentle probing, kind words and guidance, and always-intelligent responses. You have been a gift from our first conversation. My hands would shake as I returned to my manuscript, digging deeper and deeper to respond to your myriad suggestions, and each time I thought I had written the last word, I thought of you and wrote one more. Thank you from the bottom of my heart for caring as much as you did and gently guiding me as I traveled toward another awareness. What a gift you have!

Thank you to Danielle Lange for copyediting and tying the bow around my manuscript, and to Lacey Cope for creating the path to sending out my message of hope in healing. Both of you come at the time when a deep breath is due, and you have helped me take mine …. Inhale, exhale!

And finally, so much gratitude for Mindy Kuhn and Amy Ashby at Warren Publishing for taking my memoir and making it flourish. You knew exactly who would nurture my words, and I am eternally grateful. I can only hope that it makes a difference for readers to see themselves as empowered and strong, having a voice for intergenerational trauma, and healing from abuse and the challenges of loving those with mental illness.

www.ingramcontent.com/pod-product-compliance
Lightning Source LLC
Chambersburg PA
CBHW022008090426
42741CB00007B/943